GLOBETROTTER™

Travel Guide

MEXICO

W9-AAR-067

FIONA NICHOLS

NEW HOLLAND

NEW
HOLLAND

★★★ Highly recommended
★★ Recommended
★ See if you can

Third edition published in 2006
by New Holland Publishers (UK) Ltd
London • Cape Town • Sydney • Auckland
First published in 2000
10 9 8 7 6 5 4 3 2 1

website: www.newhollandpublishers.com

Garfield House, 86 Edgware Road
London W2 2EA
United Kingdom

80 McKenzie Street
Cape Town 8001
South Africa

14 Aquatic Drive
Frenchs Forest, NSW 2086
Australia

218 Lake Road
Northcote, Auckland
New Zealand

Distributed in the USA by
The Globe Pequot Press
Connecticut

ISBN 1 84537 382 0

Although every effort has been made to ensure that
this guide is up to date and current at time of going
to print, the Publisher accepts no responsibility or
liability for any loss, injury or inconvenience incurred
by readers or travellers using this guide.

Keep us Current
Information in travel guides is apt to change, which is
why we regularly update our guides. We'd be grateful
to receive feedback if you've noted something we

should include in our updates. If you have new
information, please share it with us by writing to the
Publishing Manager, Globetrotter, at the office nearest
to you (addresses on this page). The most significant
contribution to each new edition will receive a free
copy of the updated guide.

Publishing Manager (UK): Simon Pooley
Publishing Manager (SA): Thea Grobbelaar
DTP Cartographic Manager: Genené Hart
Editors: Alicha van Reenen, Melany McCallum,
Thea Grobbelaar, Sara Harper
Consultant: Dominique Adames
Picture Researchers: Shavonne Johannes, Carmen
Watts, Leigh-Anne Solomons
Design and DTP: Nicole Bannister, Éloïse Moss
Cartographers: Elmari Kuyler, Marisa Galloway,
Elaine Fick

Reproduction by Hirt & Carter (Pty) Ltd, Cape Town
Printed and bound by Times Offset (M) Sdn. Bhd.,
Malaysia.

Note: For the latest information on telephone numbers
in Mexico, see www.telmex.com.mx

Acknowledgements:
The author would like to thank the following
people for their invaluable information and
assistance: Lilian Lobato, CVB, Acapulco; Estela
Alonso, Cabo San Lucas; Guillermo Perez, Chihuahua;
Salvador Ayala, Guanajuato; David Eduardo Iturbe
Vargas, Tuxtla Gutiérrez; Dominique and Guillermo
Adames, Mexico City; Isabelle Baro, Paris, France;
Richard Koubé, Tübingen, Germany; and Fiesta
Americana and Fiesta Inn hotels.

Photographic Credits:
International Photobank/Adrian Baker: cover;
Fiona Nichols: pages 4, 7, 9, 10, 11, 12, 14, 16, 17, 20,
21, 22, 23, 24, 27, 33, 34, 37, 38, 43, 44, 45, 46, 47, 53,
55, 57, 58, 62, 66, 67, 68, 72, 78, 79 [top], 82, 87, 99,
100, 110, 115 [top], 116, 118 [top and bottom];
Neil Setchfield: pages 26, 28, 30, 41, 74, 84, 85, 86, 90,
91, 97, 98;
Mireille Vautier: title page, pages 6, 8, 13, 15, 18, 25, 29,
36, 39, 40, 42, 50, 54, 56, 65, 70, 73, 75, 76, 77, 79
[bottom], 88, 89, 94, 96, 101, 102, 103, 106, 108, 109,
111, 112, 113, 115 [bottom], 119.

Cover: *The pyramid of El Castillo, Chichén Itzá.*
Title Page: *The Maya site at Tulum, overlooking the
Caribbean.*

CONTENTS

1
Introducing
Mexico

It might take a lifetime to understand Mexico but it takes just a few days to succumb to its many charms. Vibrant and warm, varied and colourful, it is a country of immense contrasts, where a historic past resurfaces, continually piercing the pretensions of a modern world. Mexico is so near to the United States, so influenced by the economy and culture of its northern neighbour, that some degree of similarity might seem inevitable. But once south of the border territory, its own characteristics, indigenous and accumulated by years of foreign rule, become apparent. To wander through the country, stopping at will to explore its rich archaeology, its whitewashed colonial churches or its hidden shores, to sleep for a night in a hammock under clear, starry skies, and to dive into limpid tropical waters, is to start a lifelong love affair.

Many first-time visitors are lured by the promise of warm days and party nights. Their image of Mexico is of fine hotels and luxurious hideaways, temples to tourism where the adherent rarely rubs shoulders with his Mexican host. This is Mexico today, but only part of it.

The soul of Mexico – the country of cacti and riotous fiestas, of lyrical music and majestic wild scenery – is a little further away, though not out of reach. The visitor who steps out from his hotel, armed with goodwill, a guide book and a few Spanish phrases, and ventures into the small adobe villages and graceful colonial towns, will be rewarded with an experience that is hard to match elsewhere. ¡Viva Mexico!

TOP ATTRACTIONS

*** Puebla: colonial town *par excellence.*
*** Barranca del Cobre: take the Chihuahua al Pacífico train through the Canyon.
*** Palenque: see this ancient jungle city at dawn.
** Museo de Antropología: in Mexico City, one of the finest museums in the world.
** Centro Cultural Santo Domingo: in Oaxaca, an outstanding new museum.
** Baja California: watch the whales.
** Cozumel: scuba dive or snorkel off this island.

Opposite: *San Juan de Chamula, Chiapas: superstition and Christianity.*

Below: *The route between*
Durango and Mazatlán
takes in some spectacular
mountain scenery.

THE LAND

According to legend, when the conquistador Hernán
Cortés was asked by the Spanish King, Charles V, to
describe the topography of Mexico, he took a sheet of
paper, screwed it up and handed it to the king. Mexican
topography was, to Cortés at least, a series of arbitrary
mountains and valleys. Nowadays we have a better idea.

Mexico's land mass covers 1,972,551km² (761,405
sq miles). It stretches like a traditional horn from its
desert borders with the United States, through snow-
capped mountains and deep canyons to a subtropical
highland bordering Guatemala, then across to the bulb-
like Yucatán Peninsula in the east. The long finger of a
peninsula in the west, Baja California, runs parallel
with the mainland but is different in most respects.

Mountains, Lakes and Rivers

Running the length of Mexico, and forming a divide from
east to west, are the Sierra Madre mountains, called the
Sierra Madre Occidental, on the western side of the
country, and the **Sierra Madre Oriental,** which sprawl
through the central eastern parts of Mexico leaving a
swampy and humid east coast. The highest summits in
the range are the snow-capped volcanic peaks of
Orizaba at 5611m (18,410ft), **Popocatépetl** at 5452m
(17,888ft) and **Iztaccíhuatl** at 5286m (17,343ft).

Behind Acapulco and
Oaxaca the mountains
become the **Sierra Madre
del Sur** and then, as
they curl past the Gulf of
Tehuantepec, they become
the lower **Sierra Madre de
Chiapas**. In the north,
between the two sierra
ranges, lies the *altiplano* –
an area of highland with a
handful of peaks rising to
heights of around 2600m
(8531ft) or more.

In total contrast to the rest of Mexico, which is mostly mountainous, the Yucatán Peninsula is predominantly flat, relieved only by the gently rising **Puuc Hills** to the south of Mérida.

Enclosed in the hills are several lakes and lagoons. Lakes **Chapala** and **Pátzcuaro** characterize the colonial heart of the country, and attract Mexicans and visitors alike. There are several lagoons, such as **Lagunas de Montebello**, in the southern areas of the country, and parts of the Yucatán also have large lagoons, some of which hide crocodiles and all of which attract huge bird colonies.

Above: *The country's best swimming beaches are those along the Caribbean coast, specifically to the south of Playa del Carmen.*

Coasts and Islands

Over 9600km (5965 miles) of Mexico's boundaries are coastal, encompassing the Pacific Ocean, the Gulf of California, the Gulf of Mexico and the Caribbean coast. In the sheltered waters of the **Gulf of California** (also known as the Sea of Cortés), a string of small offshore islands hosts unique flora and fauna, much of which is protected in nature reserves. The Pacific coast south of Puerto Vallarta as far as the Guatemalan border is craggy and rocky with thousands of headlands, some sheltering beautiful beaches. The coral-ringed islands of **Cozumel** and **Isla Mujeres** off the Caribbean coast of the Yucatán Peninsula are popular tourist destinations.

Desert

The north of the country consists of desert. Here, in the **Desierto Sonorense** (which extends geophysically into Baja California) and **Desierto Chihuahuaense**, are the *cardón* cacti, yucca and agaves that fill our romantic images of a typical Mexican landscape. In the midst of the latter desert are the extraordinary marsh areas of **Quatro Ciénegas**.

SURFERS' PARADISE

Long known to the surfing fraternity, Puerto Escondido on the Oaxaca coast is one of the top ten surf destinations in the world. The **Mexican Pipeline** at Zicatela Beach is the big draw. The undertow is vicious and those who are not up to its strength are advised to sit it out on the beach, preferably under a *palapa* parasol, and enjoy the spectacle of the Pipeline and those who challenge its curl.

Above: *The needle-like Pachycereus cactus is a very prominent feature in parts of the barren Baja California desert.*

Climate

Mexico doesn't have one climate: it has many. The tropic of Cancer runs through the country north of Los Cabos, Mazatlán and Tampico. In the south the coast is hot and humid, while the inland areas are tempered by altitude.

Winter lasts from November to the end of March and summer from May to September, with a transitional month either side.

The northern **desert** areas receive scant rain between May and September. The temperature remains warm during the day and drops to near freezing at night for much of the year, but becomes intolerably hot (over 35°C or 95°F) in July. **Baja California** remains warm and dry year-round, with temperatures rising above 32°C (90°F) in July.

Mexico City, Guadalajara, Guanajuato and other central, **colonial cities** situated at an altitude are warmest (25–30°C or 77–86°F) between March and May, though temperatures drop considerably during winter nights. Moderate rainfall occurs here slightly later in the year.

Back on the **Pacific coast** the climate is agreeably warm throughout the year, with summer rainfall. Temperatures along the **Caribbean coast** vary very little throughout the year; daytime temperatures tend to hover around 26°C (79°F), dropping in the evening. On this coast rainfall peaks in June and September. Mérida's temperatures vary even less; they remain around 24–25°C (75–77°F) throughout the year. It can rain at any time, though the months with the heaviest rainfall are May–June and October–November.

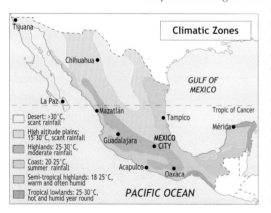

Climatic Zones

Tijuana

Chihuahua ●

GULF OF MEXICO

La Paz ●

● Mazatlán   ● Tampico   Tropic of Cancer

Mérida ●

Guadalajara   MEXICO
                      ● CITY

Acapulco ●
              Oaxaca

PACIFIC OCEAN

- Desert: >30°C, scant rainfall
- High altitude plains; 15-30°C, scant rainfall
- Highlands: 25-30°C, moderate rainfall
- Coast: 20-25°C, summer rainfall
- Semi-tropical highlands: 18-25°C, warm and often humid
- Tropical lowlands: 25-30°C, hot and humid year round

Flora and Fauna

In a country as vast and topographically varied as Mexico, there is an incredible wealth of flora and fauna. There are over 1000 bird species, 439 mammals, 989 amphibians and reptiles, and over 25,000 plants. Some of these species are found only in Mexico.

The northern reaches of Sonora, Baja California and Chihuahua are desert, but they are deserts that flower artificially. The vineyards of **Ensenada** and the wheat and cotton fields of Sonora are the result of irrigation and a lot of hard, backbreaking work.

The central mountains, the **Sierra Madre** Occidental and Oriental, are cloaked at medium altitudes with coniferous forests which peter out to scrub on the *altiplano*. These forests are the subject of much concern because of overlogging, particularly in the Barranca del Cobre region. South of Mexico City what forests remain – in an area which has been deforested and overgrazed – become more and more subtropical despite the altitude.

In the vast, flat region of the Yucatán Peninsula, once swathed in rich **tropical forests**, the wooded areas are shrinking as man makes inroads. In parts, the vegetation has been reduced to a thorny scrub, but there is still abundant plant life along some of its shoreline, where huge colonies of water birds, such as flamingos, can be found.

The last area of true **rain forest** can be found in the Lacondón Forest, Chiapas, at the Guatemalan border. These tropical and cloud forests hide a wealth of ferns and epiphytes, rare orchids, brilliantly plumed parrots and quetzals, and rare animals including monkeys and jaguars, though you will be unlikely to see many of the latter.

CUATRO CIÉNEGAS

Blue gaps in otherwise arid surroundings, this region of extraordinary rich **marshes** springing out of the Chihuahua Desert landscape has been designated a biological reserve for its unique flora and fauna. Cuatro Ciénegas ('Four Marshes') is some 200km (124 miles) from Monterrey and its unique clear water, surging from profound depths, hosts fish, turtles and other reptiles, snails and scorpions, in pools ranging from the size of a bathtub to small lakes.

Below: *Crawling through the undergrowth in Mexico are huge iguanas.*

HISTORICAL HAIRLESS HOUNDS

The **Xoloitztuintli**, sacred to the ancient Maya and Aztecs, are one of the oldest breeds of dog in the world. They are believed to date back some 3300 years. Despite being native to Mexico, these hairless dogs are very fragile and only an estimated 4000 individuals are thought to exist world-wide. The ancients attributed healing powers to these canines and used their hot blood to ease arthritic pain. What do they look like? Their skin falls in folds, they have a few clumps of hair on the head, long floppy ears, measure some 50cm (20 in) in height and weigh in at 9–14kg (20–31 lb).

Mexicans are becoming more and more aware of their natural heritage and during the course of the 20th century some 70 **national parks** and **biosphere reserves** were set up to protect areas of specific rarity or interest. Indeed, ecotourism has proved an increasing best seller and Mexicans now realize the potential of safeguarding such valuable spots.

Marine reserves have also been created to protect the offshore waters and reefs, notably those off **Cozumel** and **Isla Mujeres**, and the rich ecology of the **Bahía de Loreto** in Baja California. The reefs are also magnificent marine environments where, apart from the plethora of soft and hard corals and myriad reef fish, manta rays, sharks, turtles and dolphins are all regular visitors.

Turtles are to be found all along the coasts of Mexico. Other aquatic fauna that delight includes **sea lions** and **dolphins** (bottlenose are the most common) along much of the Pacific Coast, and **whales** – humpback, finback and grey whales. Grey whales make their way southwards to the lagoons off the western shores of Baja California where they give birth to their young between January and April each year.

HISTORY IN BRIEF

The oldest archaeological remains have been found in the central Mexican state of Puebla and date back over 20,000 years. It is believed that the early inhabitants migrated through the Bering Straits from Siberia, on a land bridge which has since become submerged, and travelled south over the millennia.

Evidence from around 6000BC suggests that these hunter-gatherers gradually became less migratory and settled into communities around the Tehuacán Valley where, according to forensic evidence, they began cultivating plants such as chillies and maize. Just three millennia later, agriculture had become a far more organized affair and villagers relied less on gathering and more on home production.

Mesoamerican Civilizations

It was in the state of Veracruz, however, that Mexico's first great civilization rose to power. The **Olmecs**, known today for their colossal basalt stone heads with stern features (the Museo de Antropología in Mexico City has examples), emerged around 1200BC in San Lorenzo, some 280km (174 miles) southeast of Veracruz. The Olmecs also centred on La Venta in Tabasco, a community which is thought to have lasted for a few centuries. We now know that apart from carving skills, which included extraordinary stone 'were-jaguars' (half human, half jaguar), the Olmecs also developed writing techniques and an advanced cosmology.

The next great civilization to evolve was that of the **Zapotecs** in Monte Albán. With an imposing site outside Oaxaca, Monte Albán grew some time after 500BC into a considerable town of 10,000 inhabitants.

Above: A legacy of Mexico's first civilization, these massive Olmec heads intrigue visitors.
Opposite: Mexico's dolphins provide a great attraction to visitors in the country's many ecological amusement areas.

EL TULE

An oddity which is well worth seeing is the huge coniferous **tree** in the churchyard at El Tule, just 10km (6 miles) outside Oaxaca. With a girth of some 50m (164ft), it is believed to be the largest of its kind in the Americas and it is thought to be well over 2000 years old – contemporary with the beginnings of the **Zapotec** civilization.

The Classical Era

The next milestone was in the 1st century AD, when **Teotihuacán** emerged as an important centre, possibly the first true urban centre in the western hemisphere. It rose to its height from AD450–650 – some 125,000 to 200,000 people are estimated to have lived there in AD500 – and declined for reasons still not clear. Archaeologists continue excavating the city (much of which is still undiscovered) and finding artefacts and human remains which increasingly piece together a picture of this once omnipotent city.

Teotihuacán probably held sway over much of the southern part of Mexico, some of Guatemala and even certain areas of Honduras. Although it was burned and looted, then abandoned, many of its practices and much of its influence continued in the centuries that followed.

HISTORICAL CALENDAR

18,500BC The first traces of human settlement.
AD450–650 The city of Teotihuacán at its height.
968–1168 The city of Tula at its height.
1370 Founding of Tenochtitlán.
1428 The Aztecs create their triple alliance.
1492 Christopher Columbus discovers America.
1502–1520 Moctezuma rules the Aztec empire.
1519 Cortés lands in Mexico.
1520 La Noche Triste.
1521 Tenochtitlán destroyed.
1522 The founding of Mexico.**1551** The creation of the University of Mexico.

1727 The annexing of Texas, California and part of Arizona.
1810 Padre Miguel Hidalgo calls for independence from the town of Dolores.
1821 The proclamation of independence.
1822 Iturbide becomes Emperor Augustín I.
1823 The abolition of the monarchy.
1861 Benito Juárez becomes president of the Republic.
1863 The French arrive in Mexico.
1864 Maximilian of Hapsburg is made Emperor.
1867 The French retreat; Maximilian is executed.

1876–1911 The Porfiriate dictatorship under Porfirio Díaz.
1910 Francisco Madero launches a move for social and agrarian reform and is elected President the following year.
1945 Start of industrialization in Mexico.
1968 Olympic Games.
1970 Mexico hosts football's World Cup.
1976 Discovery of important oil reserves.
1988 Mexico joins GATT.
1992 Mexico signs NAFTA agreement with US and Canada.
1994 The peso collapses.
1997 Hurricane Paulina ravages the Pacific coast.

Around AD300 the **Maya** began to emerge in Guatemala, moving into central Mexico. Their influence extended over 1000km (621 miles) from north to south, and 400–600km (250–373 miles) from east to west, embracing dozens of centres, some of which have only recently come to light in the thick jungle. The best preserved sites include **Palenque**, **Chichén Itzá** and **Uxmal**. The Maya organized their society around a hierarchy dominated by priests who interpreted the wishes of their gods. They refined language and gave it a written form (part phonetic, part pictorial), evolved a complex calendar which could predict eclipses of the sun and moon, and decorated their buildings with intricate art forms. What is particularly interesting is that although the great Mayan civilization is no longer with us, Mayan descendants and the language still are.

While the Maya developed their territory in southern Mexico, the **Totonacs** were building **El Tajín** near the Gulf coast. Concurrently, the **Zapotecs** were expanding **Monte Albán**. It was, in short, a period of immense growth and development which we now categorize as the 'Classical Era' in Mexican history.

It was the belligerent **Toltecs** who put an end to this era. They constructed a town just 25km (16 miles) from the ruins of Teotihuacán – **Tula** – and made their influence felt as far as the Yucatán Peninsula.

Opposite: *Intricate low relief carvings on the Temple of Quetzalcóatl.*
Below: *Temple of Warriors, one of Chichén Itzá's best-preserved monuments.*

LA MALINCHE

Doña Marina, or La Malinche, was an Indian girl whom **Cortés** took as a mistress and interpreter. She also gave birth to his children. Despite the passage of more than four centuries, La Malinche is still violently disliked – as indeed is Cortés himself – by many Mexicans, and cursed for betraying her country.

The Aztecs

At the turn of the first millennium, central Mexico was a trouble spot as a number of tribes had migrated south and sought to establish themselves. Among these were the Aztecs, who wandered into the lake-filled region around what is Mexico City today. As their legend had predicted, they saw an eagle on a cactus stump, devouring a snake, a sign which indicated that their nomadic lifestyle was over. In 1325 they started building their city, **Tenochtitlán**, and harnessed the lakes for agriculture. The city thrived, the Aztecs forged alliances with two other valley states, and over 200,000 inhabitants probably lived in Tenochtitlán and neighbouring **Tlatelolco**.

Just over two centuries later word arrived that bearded, white-skinned men had landed on their shores and were making their way inland. Moctezuma, an intellectual, was the Aztec leader at the time. His fatal mistake was to allow the Spanish to advance and ultimately he lost not only his life but also his empire.

The Conquistadors

Although Hernán Cortés and his Spanish troops landed in 1519, it was only in 1520 that they took the city of Tenochtitlán, having lost many of their number, and having massacred many more Indians in the terrible *La Noche Triste*. The following year they razed the Aztec city and set about building on its ruins their new capital, Mexico City.

Left: *A detail from a painting showing the conquistadors in the Antochiw Collection, Mexico.*
Opposite: *Aztec rituals are still played out daily in front of the Templo Mayor, Mexico City.*

The mission that the conquistadors were charged with was to assure Spanish domination of the territory, to fill Spain's coffers with gold and silver, and to establish Spanish culture and religion in Nueva España. They were largely successful in their goals, but at the expense of the local Indians. A viceroy was nominated to represent the crown in Mexico, and immigration soon followed. But Cortés' success ultimately irritated the Spanish king, who recalled him to Spain in 1540 where he lived out his life in relative obscurity.

Over the following 150 years the Spanish established dozens of towns and erected scores of religious and civic buildings, but were responsible for the decimation of the local population through disease and skirmishes. Some 2000 Spanish families migrated to the country, each receiving a land concession. In return they had to build a village church, instruct the Indians in the Catholic faith, and establish plantations for the cultivation of citrus and peach trees, cotton and sugar cane – all crops that were new to the country. Others began mining and were soon reaping the rewards of giant lodes of silver, indeed producing most of the world's silver output. Inevitably the number of Spanish *peninsulares* was soon overtaken by that of the *criollos* – the Mexicans of mixed blood.

For three centuries, the Spanish held the balance of power in Mexico, until they were undermined by one religious leader who was instrumental in ending the 300 years of colonialism.

LA NOCHE TRISTE

Many are the references to this 'Sad Night'. The night in question was between 30 June and 1 July 1520 and it has been documented in Nahuatl by the Aztecs, as well as in Spanish by the conquistadors. **Hernán Cortés** and his men had been besieged for several weeks in a palace in **Tenochtitlán**. **Moctezuma** died while in their hands, so the Aztecs attacked. Cortés had no alternative but to give the order to flee with his Indian allies under cover of night. Unwilling to quit the town without some of the riches they had accumulated, they staggered across the rain-lashed causeways, laden down with booty. An all-out battle raged and when dawn broke over Tenochtitlán, hundreds of Spanish and thousands of Indians had died. This tragedy remains in the memory of Indians throughout the country.

Above: *Miguel Hidalgo as depicted by Orozco, in the Palacio del Gobierno, Guadalajara.*
Opposite: *Pancho Villa, the great liberator and folk hero, here at Zacatecas.*

FATHER MIGUEL HIDALGO

Generally regarded as the father of Mexican independence, this priest plotted the downfall of the **Spanish regime**. Threatened with discovery, on the morning of 16 September 1810 he rang the church bells in the town of **Dolores Hidalgo** and made a speech known as the *Grito de Dolores*, calling for the people to revolt against their Spanish oppressors. This triggered the beginning of 11 years of bloody **war**. Father Hidalgo was executed in 1811, but this only served to stiffen resistance against the Spanish.

Independence and Reform

The rise of the *criollos* and an inequality in the distribution of wealth led to widespread dissatisfaction in the country. Between 1810, when Father Miguel Hidalgo uttered his famous cry for independence, and 1821 when independence was finally achieved, there was much turmoil in Mexico. It was General **Agustín Iturbide** who tipped the scales in that year, defecting from the Spanish side to that of the rebels, and it was he, indeed, who was made the first Emperor of Mexico on independence. But turbulence in the country continued and in the 30 years that followed Mexico had almost as many leaders. In 1845 the US congress voted to annex Texas and the following year the Mexican-American War broke out. The result of this was that Mexico ceded parts of New Mexico, Texas, California, Arizona, Utah and Colorado to the States. Chaos reigned and the liberals waged war against the conservatives.

It was not until **Benito Juárez** took charge with a new liberal government that matters improved. A Zapotec from Oaxaca, Juárez came to the presidency in 1861 and under him the era of **Reform** took shape.

French Intervention

In 1862, instructed to chase Mexico's bad debts with three European countries, the French landed troops and marched on Mexico City. They initially suffered defeat at Puebla but later took the city and entered the capital in 1863. Thus began French intervention, and in 1864 Napoleon III sent out **Maximilian** of Hapsburg to become emperor. His tenure only lasted three years and ended in his execution, with Juárez resuming power.

Dictatorship, Revolution and Consolidation

In 1876 a 35-year dictatorship began under **Porfirio Díaz**. It was a period of absolute rule and a semblance of order was restored, but at an appalling cost to the majority. While the rich flourished, many of the rest declined into abject poverty, living little better than serfs. Something had to give and finally, in 1910, revolution came.

It was a revolution which turned in circles: everyone was dissatisfied and, when minor victories were achieved, the leaders were found lacking. They were deposed or executed and new factions rose, with new leaders. Liberal **Francisco Madero**, legendary **Pancho Villa**, radical **Emilio Zapata**, **Alvaro Obregón**, ruthless **Victoriano Huerta**, and **Venustiano Carranza** were all important figures in this ever-shifting fight for order, justice and land reform, a decade-long battle which left dozens of leaders assassinated, thousands of ordinary people dead, and whole areas vilified.

In 1921 Obregón assumed the presidency and progress began, finally, to be made. Land was reappropriated and redistributed under Obregón's successor, **Elías Calles**, and by the time **Lázaro Cárdenas**, Mexico's singularly most popular president, had settled into his presidency, a large part of Mexico's arable lands had been redistributed. Barring the **Cristero Rebellion**, when Catholic militants rebelled at Calles' closing of many religious buildings and orders, Mexico was on a path to economic development, guided by a system that had the trappings of a democracy but was entirely authoritarian at its core.

> ### REFLECTIONS ON THE REVOLUTION
>
> 'Why did we stage a revolution? Why did we endure these miseries? We revolted for ideals so that the people would have better conditions than they had, but it is a disgrace to see that there are many wealthy people who, behind the scenes, profited from the situation while the poor still remain poor.' (**Silvestre Cadena**, revolutionary, in 1920, after nine years of fighting.)

. MÉXICO

Pronounced 'Meh Hee Ko',
the word México (which in
English we write without the
accent) comes from the
Mexica tribe, a group of
people who wandered down
from their capital city,
Aztlán, into central Mexico at
the beginning of the second
millennium and were subsequently called **Aztecs**. They
found dozens of warring city
states but this did not deter
them from establishing their
own city, **Tenochtitlán**, and
later forming an alliance with
two other city states, Texcoco
and Tlacopan, before being
decimated by the Spanish.

Below: *The lucrative salt
mines near Guerrero
Negro, Baja California,
have provoked some
major clashes between
ecologists and foreign-
owned business concerns.*

Postwar Mexico

Thanks also to the discovery of oil reserves, Mexico
developed at an ever-increasing rate after World War II
until 1968 when, along with similar unrest elsewhere,
the students marched on the street demanding the
removal of President Díaz Ordaz. It was remarkably
bad timing for the government as the Olympic Games
were about to start in Mexico City and their way of
dealing with the situation was violent. Hundreds of
students lost their lives in a battle which broke out after
a manifestation in Tlatelolco, while other left-wing
radicals were forced into hiding. Whilst things calmed
superficially, politicians were aware that their chances
of fleecing their own coffers were short-term, and
corruption mushroomed at all levels.

In 1988 Carlos Salinas de Gortari, representing the PRI
(Partido Revolucionario Institucional), assumed the
presidency and worked hard to bring about more reforms.
Under Salinas, the government released many state-
owned concerns to the private sector and, in 1994, NAFTA
(the North American Free Trade Agreement) was implemented resulting in a huge increase in *maquiladoras*
(factories working on the value-added principle, *see also*
page 19) in northern Mexico. The country seemed on the
fast track to economic stability, but it was short-lived.
Ernesto Zedillo became president, the peso crashed and
recession bit.

At the end of the
20th century Mexico
is again discontented
with the government
and economy. Crime
has risen, the number
of illegal entries into
the USA has escalated,
the movement for land
reform in Chiapas has
re-emerged and calls
for political reform are
as loud as ever.

GOVERNMENT AND ECONOMY

From an agrarian economy under a dictatorship some 90 years ago, Mexico has been transformed into an industrialized country with a demo-cratically elected president. The current leader is President Vicente Fox. The next presidential election is scheduled for July 2006. According to Mexican law a president cannot be re-elected to a second term in office.

The most important contribution to Mexico's economy was the 1994 acceptance of Mexico's membership of NAFTA, under which there is free circulation of goods and services between the two countries. Thanks in a large part to NAFTA the northern cities, such as Nuevo Léon and Monterrey, have prospered.

Petrol, **tourism** and **manufacturing** are the country's three largest revenue earners. Mexico has the fifth largest oil reserves in the world – these contribute some 10 per cent annually to the country's export earnings.

International tourism represents some 16 per cent of foreign revenue, while domestic tourism contributes some 6 per cent of the GDP.

Industrial Mexico is largely concentrated in the capital and in a radius of some 150km (93 miles) around it. Here are the car factories, food processing plants, mineral refineries and textile factories. In the northern cities are huge *maquiladoras* (factories owned by foreign concerns who import raw materials, tax-free, process them and then re-export the finished product). Mexico lured the conquistadors with rumours of mineral wealth and still remains the world's biggest producer of silver. It also mines gold and bauxite.

The **agricultural sector** is also important, and spread throughout the country, though its revenues are not proportionally high. Maize, corn, cotton, rice, beans, sugar cane and coffee figure among the most important crops, whilst livestock – cattle and pigs – are reared in the northern parts of the country.

Above: *Aztec legend prophecized that their capital city would be built where the warriors caught sight of an eagle eating a snake, while sitting atop a cactus stump. Thus they built what is now Mexico City, and the Mexican flag carries a rendition of this historic vision.*

THE METRO

Built by the French, Mexico's Metro resembles that of Paris. It is, however, **clean**, well run and **cheap**. The fare is currently around US$0.23c a ride. Routes are clearly posted and small route brochures are available. The Metro runs from 06:00–01:00 Mond–Sat, and from 07:00–01:00 Sun. During weekday rush hours, 17:30–19:30, **separate coaches** are put on trains for women so that they can avoid unwelcome male advances!

Above: *A riotous profusion of fragrant flowers, typical of Mexican markets, captured here in San Cristóbal de las Casas.*

THE PEOPLE

Historically, Mexico was a land of many tribes and civilizations and today a considerable number of their descendants still exist among the 100 million inhabitants of the country.

Over 60 per cent of Mexicans are now urban dwellers – the population of Mexico City, constantly rising, is estimated to be more than 22 million, that is over one fifth of the total population of the country – and there are also eight additional cities each with more than a million inhabitants.

Mexicans consist of an amalgam of some 20 per cent *Indígenas* – Indians who speak over 50 different languages; some 70 per cent *Mestizos* – people of mixed Indian and (mostly) Spanish origin who speak local languages and Spanish; and some 10 per cent **European** descent who are Spanish-speaking. This last group holds a disproportionately large balance of the wealth and power in the country. It is the Indians who remain largely rural while the Mestizos are drawn to city living and the hope of an easier and more lucrative life.

Travelling regionally there is a much greater chance of coming into contact with Indians, especially in small towns and at markets. In Chiapas there are still some **Mayan** descendants with their distinctive profiles, but more often you will rub shoulders with **Tzotzils**. Coastal Yucatán is still very Mayan. In Oaxaca, it is the **Zapotecs**, **Mixtecs** or Triquis. In the Yucatán, it is the Maya. In central Mexico the **Nahua** (Aztec descendants) inhabit Veracruz, San Luís Potosí and Puebla. In Michoacán (Pátzcuaro in particular), you will meet the **Purépecha**, and in Veracruz or Puebla, the **Totonacs**.

Language

The unifying language of Mexico is **Spanish**, but not the Spanish one hears in the streets of Madrid. The Spanish spoken in Mexico was brought to the country in the 16th century by adventurers from all parts of the peninsula. It was what we consider today 'old Spanish'. Add to this language a peppering of Indian words, remove the distinctive Castilian lisp and fade out the last syllable: this is Mexican Spanish. It is arguably a softer and prettier language than its mother tongue, and any attempt to speak it is greeted with enthusiasm by locals.

In addition to Spanish, some **52 languages** are spoken by the indigenous Indian population, some of whom understand no Spanish at all.

> **MASTERING SPANISH**
>
> **Cuernavaca** is one of the most popular places (along with San Miguel de Allende, Guanajuato, Guadalajara and Puerto Vallarta) to learn Spanish. The minimum length of a course is a week (the usual enrolment is for four weeks) and schools can arrange student accommodation with the local families. Contact the **Cuernavaca Anglo Americano**, tel/fax: (73) 17-2210.

Religion

The conquering Spanish found a variety of cultures, all with different religious practices. Wherever the conquistadors went in pursuit of mineral riches, the clergy followed in search of souls. In the name of Catholicism they set about converting the Indians to the 'true faith' and in the process massacred many. During the centuries that followed there was an uneasy cohabitation between the church and the crown, as both amassed vast riches, and by the time of independence the church's influence was curtailed.

Today the vast majority of Mexican people embrace Christianity, and predominantly **Catholicism**. A small minority, however, still incorporate some Indian elements in their Christianity. Interestingly, the *curanderos* (healers) and *brujos* (witches) still have a following in parts of the country.

Below: *The modern cathedral in Acapulco epitomizes the city's forward-looking attitudes.*

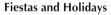

FESTIVALS

The most important annual events in Mexico are:
5 February • *Día de la Constitución:* Constitution Day. Commemorating the signing of Mexico's constitution.
Mid-February or early March • *Carnaval:* Carnival. The week prior to Lent.
March or April • *Semana Santa:* Holy Week.
5 May • *Cinco de Mayo:* national holiday recalling Mexico's defeat of the French in Puebla.
16 September • *Día del Independencia:* the most important holiday. In Mexico City the masses converge on the *zócalo* to hear the president affirm the famous *grito*, or cry for independence.

Fiestas and Holidays

Apart from the major national festivals, many others are celebrated in Mexico. These include **New Year's Day**, **Día de los Reyes Magos** (Day of the Three Kings, 6 January) or Epiphany when children receive gifts, and **Día de la Candelería** (Candlemas, 2 February), with bullfights and processions, particularly in Veracruz.

Día de Nacimiento de Benito Juárez (21 March) is the anniversary of Juárez' birthday and a national holiday. The **Spring Equinox** is marked at Chichén Itzá in an extraordinary phenomenon of light on architecture. **Good Friday**, **Holy Saturday** and **Easter Sunday** are all holidays.

On 1 May, **Día de Trabajo** (May Day) is fêted with parades in Mexico City. **Fiesta de Corpus Christi** (66 days after Easter) is particularly interesting in Paplanta, Veracruz and Mexico City. **Fiesta de San Juan el Bautista** (the feast of St John the Baptist, 24 June) is a national holiday, likewise **Fiesta de la Virgen de la Carmen** (16 July).

Día de la Raza (Day of the Race, 12 October) celebrates Columbus' discovery of the New World. **Días de los Muertos** (All Saints' and All Souls' Days, 1 and 2 November) are when the souls of the dead are said to return to earth. The best celebrations are at Pátzcuaro. **Anniversario de la Revolución** (20 November) marks the anniversary of the 1910 Revolution.

Día de Nuestra Señora de Guadalupe (12 December) is the feast day of Mexico's patron saint, Our Lady of Guadalupe. There are festivities throughout the country but particularly at the Iglesia de Nuestra Señora de Guadalupe in Mexico City and at Puerto Vallarta in the church of Our Lady of Guadalupe. **Las Posadas** (16-24 December) represent the twelve days of Christmas. Celebrated nationwide with candlelit processions, reenacting Mary and Joseph's search for shelter. This is particularly beautiful in Querétaro. Lastly, **Día del Navidad** (25 December) is Christmas Day.

Dance

For those whose visits don't coincide with major Indian festivals, scheduled dance performances are the easiest way to get a feel for Mexican dance. The **Ballet Folklórico** in Mexico City is a highly professional introduction to this art and shouldn't be missed. Similar, but less extensive, companies often perform in Guadalajara, Puerto Vallarta and Acapulco.

Above: *Mexico's folklore, often inaccessible, is brought to its visitors through stunning performances such as this one.*
Opposite: *Participants in the Carnival parade at Huejotzingo.*

Music

Mexico has a rich musical heritage, fuelled by its position between the USA and Latin America, creating a vibrant mixture of styles. From Mariachi to *Norteño*, Afro-Caribbean rhythms and American rock, there is something for everyone. The traditional songs of each region are generally a fusion of Indian and Spanish cultures.

Archaeology and Fine Art

Evidence of the talents of early Mexicans is still around: the massive Olmec heads in Villahermosa are over 2000 years old; the stylized Toltec figures at Tula over 1000; so too the frescoes in Palenque and the bas reliefs in Chichén Itzá. The **Museo Nacional de Antropología** in Mexico City puts some of the best works under one roof.

The architectural contribution of Spain forms part of Mexico's heritage. Cities like Puebla, San Miguel de Allende, Guadalajara, Oaxaca, San Cristóbal de las Casas, Mérida or Zacatecas are living showcases. They brought their silversmiths, sculptors, muralists and painters to decorate the interiors of churches and civil buildings, and these masters gradually trained the local artists. By the 19th and early 20th century the arts embraced both Spanish and Mexican elements. The **Pinacoteca Virreinal**

THE CLOUD PEOPLE

High up in the mountains of the **Sierra Madre del Sur**, where the evening fog clouds the vistas, lives a group of people who have inhabited the region for over a thousand years. Neither Maya nor Aztec, the Cloud People, as they call themselves, are Mixtec and Zapotec. They live in the state of **Oaxaca**, the state with the largest diversity of ethnic population groups. There are estimated to be over 340,000 **Zapotecs** and 240,000 **Mixtecs** in the state.

de San Diego in Mexico City is an excellent place to get an idea of painting during the colonial era.

The so-called **Churrigueresque style**, a highly ornate way of decorating buildings (named for Catalan architect José de Churriguera), is a peculiar Mexican characteristic and one which you find in many colonial towns.

In the 1920s Mexico's greatest art form was the mural, commissioned to commemorate the country's history and to reflect its changes. Its three greatest exponents – **Diego Rivera**, **José Clemente Orozco** and **David Alfaro Siqueiros** – marked the debut of modern Mexican art.

Other great artists include **Frida Kahlo**, painter **Remedios Vara**, muralist **Juan O'Gorman** and Zapotec **Rufino Tamayo**, a postwar muralist from Oaxaca. **Pedro Ramírez Vásquez** and **Luís Barragan** are probably Mexico's best-known modern architects.

Arts and Crafts

Mexico has a rich and diverse range of *artisanerías* (handicrafts), particularly in regions with large Indian populations. Many towns have a **Casa de Artisanías** which gives a good idea of local products, while the largest cities offer handicrafts from all parts of the country. Markets, too, are a good place to buy, but bargaining skills are important.

Textiles are perhaps the best-known handicrafts. Traditional clothing, such as blouses, *huipiles* (tunics), serapes, sashes, blankets and bags, abounds in rural areas. So too, hammocks. **Leather** bags, belts, sandals, boots, even hats, are a feature of northern Mexico and are often available at prices well below those one is used to paying.

Jewellery, especially silverware, is a Mexican tradition and can be found in all shopping malls and hotel lobbies. Taxco is *the* place to buy and the range of goods is vast. Look out for mirrors in silver frames. Oaxaca and Puerto Vallarta are also known for their gold jewellery.

Lacquerware is a continuing tradition. Gourds are often used as the base for bright paintings and designs. **Wooden figures**, animals, toys, puppets, guitars and furniture (reputable companies can ship goods) all make interesting mementos. **Masks**, made from wood or papier-mâché, are also a popular souvenir of traditional dances. **Paintings** are another popular form of handicraft. Bark paintings, an old tradition, come from San Pablito, in the state of Puebla.

Ceramics and **pottery** are functional and decorative. The Spanish arrived in Mexico with their *talavera* goods, and this style was copied in Puebla and Dolores Hidalgo. Near Oaxaca unusual black pottery, decorated with incisions, is produced by the locals, while the Guadalajara suburbs of Tonalá and Tlaquepaque are renowned for a variety of ceramics, furniture, glassware and woodwork.

BARGAINING
It is essential to bargain for goods in markets. There is no hard-and-fast rule as to the amount by which you should reduce the asking price – you have one of two options. The first is to decide how much the item is worth *to you*. Then state a figure **lower** than your price. The game now starts. The vendor will then make a **counter-offer**. You make another and so on until the vendor won't move further. The second option is harder but usually more successful. Each time the vendor states a price, you ask, politely, for a better one. Until a price that is acceptable is arrived upon, you continue politely to ask the vendor for a lower price. If they lose interest, then the true price of the item is probably their last one.

Opposite: *Not to be missed, the Capilla del Rosario in the church of Santo Domingo, Puebla, is a marvellous example of gilt Baroque style.*
Left: *Painting on bark is an unusual but fascinating tradition.*

Sport and Recreation

With such a varied topography, largely temperate climate and unpolluted, warm seas, it is not surprising that Mexico offers a wide variety of world-class sporting options. Many of its newer sights are, indeed, hands-on experiences with nature.

A relative newcomer to **golf**, the country now boasts scores of fine signature golf courses in some wonderful locations. For instance, Los Cabos has six magnificent (and sometimes rather expensive!) courses along the Corridor, and Acapulco has five outstanding choices, from Revolcadero back into the heart of town. Puerto Vallarta, Ixtapa and Huatulco all have golf courses.

In all the resort destinations, holiday-makers can play **tennis** (all the new resorts boast fine courts), go horseback riding and take care of their form in state-of-the-art **gyms** and **spas**. **Parasailing**, (hanging onto a parachute and being towed by a speedboat) is immensely popular, and viewing such spectacular bays as those of Acapulco or Puerto Vallarta from the air is an unforgettable experience.

Horseback riding enthusiasts can also explore a number of areas, including the Barranca del Cobre, on horseback. The more energetic can **hike** or walk around several archaeological sites or in the country's many national parks, from the volcanic areas in central Mexico to the Montebello lagoons near the southern border.

While land sports are a great lure, Mexico's watersports are tops. Renowned for its **diving**, Cozumel is one of the best – and favourite – dive destinations. Indeed, the shores all around the northeastern part of the Yucatán are excellent scuba and **snorkelling** territory. Competent dive schools offer facilities for

certified divers or courses for the novice. Snorkellers, too, revel in the fabulous lagoons such as Xel-Há or Chankanaab in the Yucatán. There is good diving, too, along the Pacific and in Baja California, especially around Los Cabos and La Paz. Baja is noted for its **sea kayaking**. The eastern shores (bordering the Sea of Cortés) are often shallower and calmer, providing the ideal conditions for exploring the rich marine environment and offshore islands. Fishing, too, is one of Mexico's great attractions. Baja California is one of the world's finest spots for hooking marlin, sailfish or tuna.

Charreadas and Bullfights

The ***charreada***, Mexico's version of a rodeo, is held on Sundays all over the country and particularly in Guadalajara. Here the brave take on wild steers and unbroken horses, demonstrate roping techniques and strut before a lively crowd. It is from the *charreadas* that Mexican dress – tight black trousers with silver studs, short jacket and wide-brimmed hat – took its form.

Imported from Spain, **bullfighting** is another popular weekend and fiesta event in Mexico, particularly big in the north of the country.

Above: *Bullfighting is a popular sport with locals, especially during festivals, when they attract crowds.*
Opposite: *Parasailing in places such as Puerto Vallarta affords alternative views of Mexico's coast.*

LUCHA LIBRE

A national sport, the *Lucha Libre* is a form of free-for-all **wrestling**. The difference is that the protagonists wear decorated **masks** that give them an identity of their own. Audience participation is very active and there is a great atmosphere. There are bouts each Thursday, Friday and Saturday evening in **Mexico City**. Both the Arena Coliseo and Arena México are in the centre of town.

Food and Drink

Mexico is responsible for some of our favourite European ingredients. Tomatoes, beans, sweet potatoes and chocolate (not to mention tobacco) were all part of the varied Mayan and Aztec cuisine. The Spanish pined, however, for familiar ingredients and soon brought oil, vinegar, wine, spices, cheese and livestock to recreate a more familiar diet. Thus a culinary marriage of new and old worlds was wrought. It was further expanded when the French brought their savoir-faire in 1862. And, thanks to the United States, fast food is now everywhere in Mexico.

Corn is the basic ingredient for most Mexican meals. The Maya believed it was a divine gift and as such venerated it. Today, it is used mainly for *tortillas* (Mexico's answer to bread and an essential accompaniment to a meal), for *tacos* (crispy tortillas filled with meat, fish or vegetables and the nation's most popular snack) and for *enchiladas* (soft tortillas filled with meat or chicken, lettuce, sour cream and more). In regions where wheat replaces corn as the staple crop, flour tortillas are created instead and, filled with savoury goodies, become *burritos*.

There are more than 100 varieties of **chilli**. Not all chillies are devastatingly hot like the *habanero* – some are rich and sweet. Chillies appear in most cooked dishes while a small bowl of chilli salsa – a mix of tomato, coriander, onion and chilli – is offered as a condiment. Other predominant ingredients in the cuisine are green limes, coriander, cumin, chickpeas, squash and garlic.

While Spain has its *tapas*, Mexico has its *antojitos* – a snack or light dish offered to accompany a beer. It could be *chorizo* sausage, *queso fundido*, melted cheese on tortillas, peanuts, or stuffed peppers – they are all tasty nibbles designed to give you a thirst.

Stewed or fried (*refritos*) *frijoles*, or **beans**, are an integral part of a Mexican meal and provide a poor population with both protein and fibre. **Rice** is the other constant staple. Mostly made with cow's milk, **cheese** is a much-used basis for meals: grated, baked and melted in a wide range of dishes. Europeans tend to find the cheeses rather bland.

Tequila and **beer** are the most famous Mexican drinks. **Mezcal** and **pulque** alcohols are also made from the cactus plant, but by different processes. Beers (Corona, Sol, Carta Blanca, Dos Equis, Victoria, Negra Modelo, Bohemia and Indio) are found throughout the country and often drunk from the bottle through a slice of lemon. **Wine** lovers will find that red wines from the Ensenada and Zacatecas areas are very palatable and not particularly expensive.

Along the tropical coastline, *licuados* (sweetened water and fruit juices) and *jugos* (squeezed fruit juices) are delicious thirst quenchers. Buy freshly made ones. For something a bit stronger, **Mexican rum**, especially *anejo* (aged rum), made from local sugar cane, is good. **Kahlúa**, the coffee liqueur, is also a popular Mexican drink. Lastly, bottled **mineral water** is widely available and a must in a country without potable tap water.

REGIONAL SPECIALITIES

In Mexico City, Acapulco, Los Cabos, Puerto Vallarta or Cancún, cuisine has no frontiers. Elsewhere, regional dishes and Mexican favourites fill menus. In the central states, Aztec and Spanish ingredients form dishes such as *mole poblano* and *chiles en nogada*. Further south, the Maya thrived on *tamales* (stuffed, steamed corn husks), still common in Chiapas.

The Yucatán has its own style of tropical cuisine. Bananas play an important role: try chicken or fish steamed in banana leaves. Veracruz and Quintana Roo are known for fish and sea-foods which are sometimes (like *ceviche*) marinated in lime or simply grilled; the Pacific Coast, too, serves up plenty of fish and seafood.

In the north, cowboy country, **steak** is very good. And, as wheat is the pre-dominant grain, tortillas are made of wheat flour.

For the sweet tooth, there are plenty of *pasteles* and *dulces* (sugary concoctions and cakes), and breakfast will often consist of a *dulce* and milky coffee. Then there are regional **fruits** galore, all of which must be thoroughly washed before eating.

Opposite: *Along with tequila, Mezcal is a popular liquor in Mexico.*
Left: *Tortillas are the staple for all Mexican meals.*

2
Mexico City and Environs

More than 22 million people call Mexico City home, and that figure rises by 2000 daily as more seek work in the capital. It is simply one of the most crowded places on earth. But what a place!

Mexico Ciy lies at an altitude of 2240m (7349ft), sprawling across the 7800km² (3011 sq miles) Valley of Mexico. When Cortés arrived it was a beautiful area of lakes, trees, flowers and impressive towns, but today Mexico City extends annually towards the snow-capped volcanoes Popocatépetl and Iztaccíhuatl that were, not so long ago, scores of kilometres from the urban mass.

Mexico City is divided into 16 *delegaciones*, each subdivided into *colonias*. Getting around a city this size requires planning and should, as a generalization, be done by day. Taxis, buses, *pesero* minibuses and the metro cover most of the city and the smart visitor divides his sightseeing into areas, tackling one at a time.

To talk of pollution, congestion, crime and subsidence – four problems which preoccupy the citizens of Mexico City – is to dwell on the negative side of the capital. The appeal of the city lies in its wealth: social, historical and cultural. Mexicans are warm people, pleased to share their city with visitors and delighted in their interest.

Located in the heart of the country, Mexico City is an ideal setting-out point for destinations elsewhere in Mexico. Easily accessible for a day trip are many well-preserved colonial cities, such as **Taxco** and **Puebla**, and fascinating archaeological sites, including **Teotihuacán**, one of the most impressive ruined cities in the world.

DON'T MISS

*** Museo Nacional de Antropología: one of the world's best museums.
*** Puebla: national heritage and beautiful colonial town.
*** Teotihuacán: massive pyramids and ancient city.
** Cuernavaca: resort town, home of the rich and famous.
** Taxco: the silver capital.
** Templo Mayor: historic remains of the Aztec's capital.
** Zócalo: vast open plaza in the heart of Mexico City.
* Palacio de Bellas Artes: the Ballet Folklórico, an expression of Mexican culture seen in dance and music.

Opposite: *Mexico City has some rather unusual modern architecture.*

CLIMATE

This is an area of wet summers and moderate temperatures. Mexico City is on a **tropical** latitude but, because it is at such a high altitude, its climate is fairly gentle, generally being spring-like year-round. Pollution is at its highest during winter, with day temperatures around 20°C (68°C), dropping to 7°C (45°F) at night. Summers may be humid but less polluted. Day temperatures average 26° or 27°C (79° to 81°F) in April and May (the hottest months) but can drop quite sharply at night.

Opposite: *A bird's-eye view of Mexico City's vast Zócalo and Cathedral.*

CENTRO HISTÓRICO

Mexico City was founded on what remained of Tenochtitlán, the Aztec city that Cortés destroyed. The **Zócalo** and **Catedral** were built here, and this is the best place to start any visit because it incorporates elements of all eras and is the heart of Mexico City. Note that most museums are closed on Mondays.

The Zócalo ★★

The word *zócalo* comes from the Aztec and means 'stone base'. It was first used to describe this huge plaza, over 200m (219yd) on each side, built with Aztec stones on what was the Aztecs' own Plaza Mayor, or main square. In colonial days it was used as the main market but today it is the gathering point for the disgruntled or rallying point for celebrations such as Independence Day in September.

The *Zócalo* is also the governmental heart. The **Palacio Nacional**, on the eastern side of the square, houses the presidential offices, the treasury and **Diego Rivera's** magnificent murals depicting the history of Mexico (it is open to the public and one identification document per group is required). From a balcony here on 15 September each year – the eve of Independence Day – the President utters the famous *Grito de Dolores*,

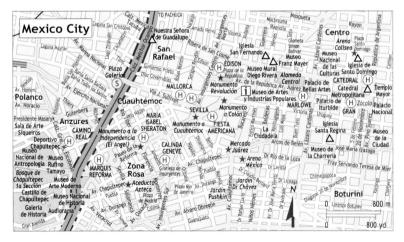

affirming Padre Miguel Hidalgo's 1810 cry for independence.

Catedral Metropolitana ★★

The oldest and largest cathedral in Latin America was begun in the late 16th century, but its wide façade with twin towers and the neo-Classical dome date from the 19th century. Inside, the once magnificent decorative elements are, sadly, masked by dense green scaffolding which holds up the whole subsiding cathedral, but some of the 14 chapels along the side naves and the richly decorated **Capilla de los Reyes**, reserved for the elite, still offer a glimpse of its former grandeur. The **Sagrario**, a separate parish church, lies to the east of the cathedral. It is not open to the public but its highly ornate Churrigueresque exterior is well worth seeing.

Templo Mayor ★★

It was only in the 1970s that this historic Aztec building, lying to the north of what is now the *Zócalo*, was discovered by accident and subsequently excavated. This was the Aztecs' principal temple, one dedicated to Huitzilopochtli and Tláloc, the gods of, respectively, war and rain, and one in which thousands of **human sacrifices** were made. The temple is thought to have been erected on the site where the Aztecs saw their eagle and snake on top of a cactus – still the symbol of Mexico today – and was an amalgam of a number of successive buildings. The excavated site is rather confusing to the layman, and it is far more fruitful to spend time in the excellent **museum** where a collection of fabulous artefacts, such as the sacrificial stone carved with a relief of the moon goddess, Coyolxauhqui, trace the history and culture of the Aztecs.

HOY NO CIRCULA

Each week, car-driving citizens of Mexico City have to forego using their car for one weekday to help reduce the **pollution** levels, unless their vehicle is brand new. This is determined by the digits on each **licence plate**. When pollution levels rise above acceptable (for Mexico City) levels, a two-day restriction on driving is implemented. The wealthier citizens get around the problem by renting or buying a **second car** with different number plates.

Above: *A Baroque gem, the magnificent Palacio de Bellas Artes is the venue for the Ballet Folklórico and other spectacles.*

Museums and Churches

In **Calle Moneda**, the old government mint now houses the **Museo Nacional de las Culturas**, with art from around the world. Nearby, don't miss the **Museo José Cuervas**, with superb paintings by Cuervas and other modern Latin-American artists; the Baroque **Palacio del Arzobispado**; the Churrigueresque **Iglesia de la Santísima** and Diego Rivera's murals in the **Museo de San Ildefonso**. Before going to the **Alameda**, a detour to the **Plaza** and **Iglesia de Santo Domingo** offers a glimpse of colonial Mexico.

AROUND ALAMEDA PARK

Running between the *Zócalo* and Alameda Central, **Avenida Madero** is, in parts, reserved for pedestrians – a delight in this congested city. The impressive Baroque **Palacio de Iturbide** (free entrance) is probably Mexico's finest mansion. You cannot miss the modern **Torre Latinoamericana** which pierces the polluted skies with its 47 storeys. On a good day the views from its observation deck are stunning. Also hard to miss is the blue and white tiled façade of the **Casa de los Azulejos** on Avenida Madero. Consider having lunch in its restaurant and enjoy the building at the same time. Don't miss the Orozco frescoes.

Palacio de Bellas Artes ★

East of Alameda Park is the white marble **Palacio de Bellas Artes**. Here are extensive murals and paintings by Rivera, Orozco, Siqueiros and Tamayo. The Palacio also houses the large **Teatro de Bellas Artes** where not only concerts and operas are staged but also the thrice-weekly **Ballet Folklórico de México** – a must for all visitors.

Mexico's main post office, the **Correos**, commissioned by Porfirio Díaz, is another striking monument built of snowy white marble. It also houses a museum.

More Museums

An impressive mansion on Avenida Tacuba, modelled on Italian Renaissance palaces, the **Museo Nacional de Arte** houses a wonderful collection of Mexican paintings, amongst which are works by Velasco depicting a tranquil Valley of Mexico, long since disappeared. Opposite, the neo-Classical **Palacio de Minería** houses meteorites. For folk art, the renovated **Museo de Artes y Industrias Populares**, south of Alameda, and the **Museo Mural Diego Rivera**, on the western side, are both worth a detour.

Paseo de la Reforma ★★

Emperor Maximilian commissioned the Paseo de la Reforma to connect the Alameda with his palace in **Chapultepec Park**. It used to be a *champs élysées* lined with colonial buildings, but today it is an eight-lane thoroughfare punctuated by *glorietas* (traffic circles), and has become a monument to modern architecture with its glassy skyscrapers, embassies, luxury hotels and nearby smart Zona Rosa. Nevertheless it is fascinating to explore.

Zona Rosa ★

Smart shoppers and diners head for the Zona Rosa, the place to see and be seen, although other neighbourhoods are now vying for this distinction. Here are **cinemas**, **boutiques**, **restaurants** and **cafés** for all tastes. It is not cheap to stay here, but all facilities, including banks, airlines, the US Embassy and the Tourist Office, are in the neighbourhood. The Zona Rosa gives way to Condesa, not only a middle-class neighbourhood that is enjoying a new popularity with the in-crowd, but also a *colonia* graced with decent parks such as **Parque México**.

WHAT'S OPEN ON MONDAYS?

Practically all **museums** are **closed on Mondays**, but here is a list of **places** that are **open to visitors:**
• Palacio Nacional (Diego Rivera murals)
• Nacional Monte de Piedad (the enormous and fascinating pawnshop)
• Museo de Medicina Mexicana
• Casa de los Azulejos (Sanborn's restaurant)
• Torre Latinoamericana
• Palacio de Iturbide
• Museo de San Carlos (European art)
• Basílica de Guadalupe
• Cathedral
• Xochimilco
• Daily markets

Turibus: Circuito Turistico is an all-day hop-on-hop-off tour of the city. It departs from the Auditorio metro station exit, in front of the Auditorio itself.

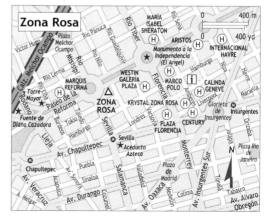

AMUSING THE CHILDREN

Chapultepec Park is a great place for children to let off steam and see some less adult sights. The **Parque Zoológico** (open 09:00–16:00 Tue–Sun) has a fine collection of animals. And the Museum in the Castle has interesting armour. Take the older children past the **Monumento a los Niños Héroes**, the monument to the six brave boys who defended their military academy to the end and finally leapt to their deaths. Then proceed to the **Papalote Museo del Niño**, a very popular and highly successful Children's Museum. **Chapultepec Mágico** is an excellent amusement park, while the **Technological Museum** has hands-on exhibits. Older children may also enjoy the **Museo de Minería**, or Mining Museum, with its minerals and machinery.

CHAPULTEPEC PARK

Recreational area for Aztec nobles, lungs for the modern-day city, Chapultepec Park is an important leisure and cultural focus in Mexico City and on Sundays teems with Mexicans toying with footballs or dozing in hammocks. The **Monumento a los Niños Héroes** commemorates six cadets who, in 1847, defended their military academy to the last against the invading Americans and chose to leap to their deaths rather than surrender.

Chapultepec Park is the location of three important **museums**, including the world-renowned Museum of Anthropology (*see* opposite page), as well as Castillo de Chapultepec and a number of monuments.

Museo Rufino Tamayo ★

This museum contains an excellent collection of works amassed by the great Zapotec artist, Tamayo. It also includes works by Picasso, Miró and Moore, as well as by important Mexican painters.

Castillo de Chapultepec ★

This castle was built on the site of the Aztec Summer Palace by the Spanish Viceroy in 1785 and served, briefly, as the main residence for Emperor Maximilian

and his wife, Charlotte (Carlotta). Their furnished apartments are open to visitors. The castle also houses the **Museo Nacional de Historia** which puts much of Mexican history into perspective. There are some major exhibits of weaponry, armour, coins, furniture and books which cover the period from the Spanish Conquest to the Revolution.

Museo Nacional de Antropología ★★★

This is probably the most important museum of its type in Mexico, if not in the Americas, and it needs a lot of time, preferably over a number of visits, for visitors to absorb both its archaeological and ethnographic exhibits. The latter are often overlooked but deserve equal praise for their wonderful presentation.

Pedro Ramírez Vásquez designed the superb building. With over 5km (3 miles) of exhibits, it was completed in 1964 and was extensively renovated in 2000.

The **Sala de Orientación** offers a 45-minute audiovisual display of Mexican history encapsulating much of what the museum covers. A museum plan indicates which areas hold the most interest for a visitor:

Origins Room: this room contains recent excavations and special exhibits.

Pre-Classic Room: exhibits from 1500BC to AD250.

Teotihuacán Room: here are models of the city, as well as a full-scale reconstructed model of a section of the Temple of Quetzalcóatl.

Toltec Room: contains the civilizations in central Mexico in the years from AD650–1250.

Mexican Room: this room is devoted to the Mexica tribe, or Aztecs. This covers Tenochtitlán.

Oaxaca Room: Zapotec achievements from 300BC to AD700 and the Mixtecs, from AD1200–1500.

Gulf of Mexico Room: a room devoted to the Olmecs, Totonac and Huastec civilizations.

Maya Room: contains exhibits not only from Mexico but also from Guatemala, Belize and Honduras.

Northern Room: this room is devoted to the sites in far northern Mexico, and also Chihuahua.

Western Room: cultures of the west, in Jalisco, Colima, Nayarit and Michoacán, including those of the Purépecha. If you are not travelling to Papantla or El Tajín, don't miss the **voladores**, or fliers, who perform their rites several times a day near the museum's entrance.

Above: *The voladores unwind themselves outside the Museo de Antropología.*

Opposite: *Sundays are the best time for relaxing in Chapultepec Park.*

HIGHLIGHTS OF THE MUSEO DE ANTROPOLOGÍA

- Decorated Aztec **solar calendar** stone
- **Costumes** of many of the indigenous tribes
- Massive stone statue of **Quetzalcóatl** from Tula
- Huge stone **Olmec heads**
- Mayan **death masks**
- The statue of a bearded **human head** in the mouth of a **coyote**, executed in terracotta and shell
- The 3000-year-old **acrobat sculpture** from Tlatilco

POLANCO

A smart suburb just north of Chapultepec, Polanco has a plethora of restaurants, art galleries, shops, hotels and a couple of museums. It is the best place to shop in the capital. The home of muralist **David Siquieros** is now a museum, housing a collection of his works and private documents. Also in Polanco is the **Centro Cultural Arte Contemporáneo**, a collection of ultramodern art which elicits a varied response from visitors.

COYOACÁN AND SAN ÁNGEL

Once a colonial town in its own right (Cortés lived here at one time), Coyoacán is now a colonial suburb bordering San Ángel. Here is located the **Museo Léon Trotsky**, where the famous Russian lived for a period of three years before being assassinated.

Another interesting place to visit is the **Museo de las Culturas Populares**, which includes a history of Mexico's popular culture and exhibitions on *lucha libre* (freestyle masked wrestling), nativity models and rituals for the *Día de los Muertos* (All Souls' Day).

Trendy San Ángel holds the famous **Bazaar Sábado** each Saturday, in its **Plaza San Jacinto**. The market offers plenty of folk art and handicrafts and it is an excellent reason to come and explore this delightful suburb full of cobbled streets, small galleries and museums. Its **Museo Casa Estudio Diego Rivera y Frida Kahlo**, the studio of muralist Rivera and his much younger wife, artist Frida Kahlo, also attracts many visitors. Its cubist architecture is quite fascinating and the museum provides an insight into the lives of this extraordinary couple.

DIEGO AND FRIDA

An extraordinary couple they made! **Diego Rivera** (sometimes called the 'giant frog') was 21 years older than his crippled and diseased wife, **Frida Kahlo**. They lived side by side in two separate houses in the **San Ángel** area of Mexico City. While he painted some of Mexico's greatest murals, such as his autobiographical *Sueño de una Tarde de Domingo en la Alameda* (Dream of a Sunday Afternoon in the Alameda) housed in the Museo Mural Diego Rivera, the beautiful Kahlo led a life of pain, seeking solace in her painting and an unconventional lifestyle. During their time in her 'Blue House' they hosted such luminaries as **Trotsky**, with whom Kahlo had said to have had an affair.

GREATER MEXICO CITY

The valley of Mexico must have been stunning, with its tree-covered hills, extensive lakes and floating islands, and a visit to the floating gardens of **Xochimilco**, south of Mexico City, harks back to those days. The Aztecs mastered the art of growing flowers and produce on floating rafts (*chinampas*) and what remains today are self-anchored rafts. Visitors rent narrow boats for a ride, often serenaded by passing Mariachi bands, through the canals.

Xochimilco is also the home of the **Museo Dolores Olmedo Patiño**, a museum housing Señora Olmedo's private collection of works by Rivera.

In the northern suburbs of Mexico City, the **Basílica de Nuestra Señora de Guadalupe**, dedicated to the country's patron saint, is Mexico's most important religious monument. Built in 1536 but later much modified, the Basilica is sinking into the soft subsoil. In 1976 Vázquez was commissioned to build the modern sanctuary, a steel and glass structure, and it is to this that today's pilgrims make their way, often completing the last steps on their knees.

North of the Alameda is the **Plaza de Tres Culturas**. Here converge the Aztec pyramids of Tlatelolco, the Spanish **Iglesia de Templo de Santiago** and modern **Secretaría de Relaciones Exteriores**, marking Mexico's three cultures.

CHINAMPAS

The Aztecs created a series of natural **barges** (*chinampas*) out of poles, wood and lake soil and, by fastening them together, formed a **pontoon**, enabling them to get from one island area to the next. They also used these *chinampas* to create **gardens**, planting the rafts with flowers and vegetables and punting them around from sun to shade according to the plants' requirements. The floating gardens of **Xochimilco**, now firmly anchored by willow trees, are the legacy of this unusual form of horticulture.

Opposite: *Part of Diego Rivera's fabulous murals in the Palacio Nacional.*
Below: *Xochimilco's Floating Gardens are one of the city's fun places, especially on weekends.*

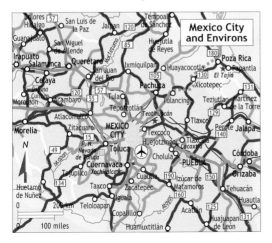

NORTH AND NORTHEAST OF MEXICO CITY

To the north and northeast of Mexico City are Tula and Teotihuacán – two of the country's most celebrated archaeological sights. The colonial town of Tepotzotlán is also well worth a visit.

Tepotzotlán ★★★

A small colonial town 43km (27 miles) north of Mexico City, Tepotzotlán has one of the most beautiful examples of Churrigueresque-style architecture in the country. Its **Iglesia de San Francisco Javier** was started in the late 17th century and finished in the 18th. Not only is its façade a symphony in Baroque but its amazingly intricate carved interior defies description. No expense was spared on the gilt carvings, the sculpted cherubs or the numerous saints. Visit the **Museo Nacional del Virreinato**, housed in the 16th-century monastery, for more religious artefacts, folk art and fine art treasures.

Tula ★★

The ruins of the great Toltec city, Tula (Tollán), lie 96km (60 miles) north of Mexico City. This militaristic city was at its height during the period AD900–1200 but was conquered by the Aztecs in the 14th century. Some of the Toltec rituals, including mass human sacrifice to appease the gods, were subsequently incorporated into Aztec culture.

Not to be missed is the **Pirámide de Quetzalcóatl**, topped by its four *atlantes*, enormous carved stone columns that must have held a roof at one time. Next to the pyramid, set amid a scattering of pillars and columns, are two

Left: *Spectacular views of the Pyramid of the Sun, Teotihuacán.* **Opposite:** *These impressive Toltec heads still stand at Tula.*

OBSIDIAN

Obsidian was mined at **Cerro de las Navajas** – Mountain of the Knives – north of **Teotihuacán**, and it was thanks to this mineral that Teotihuacán became such an economic success. A fragile but immensely sharp natural glass, obsidian was fashioned into scrapers, knives or spears and used by tribes throughout Central America.

chac mool sculptures, those reclining figures in which the centre is in the form of a bowl for human hearts. Near the site entrance is a **Juego de Pelota**, or ball court (there is a second one beyond the other main buildings).

Teotihuacán ★★★

About 50km (31 miles) to the northeast of central Mexico City lies one of the greatest archaeological marvels in Mexico and its largest ancient city – Teotihuacán. At its peak in the 6th century AD, over 150,000 people lived in this great city of 24km² (9 sq miles), many of them involved in mining obsidian. Then, sometime in the 7th century it declined, was plundered and finally abandoned. However, the later Toltecs and Aztecs still revered the sacred site. The Aztecs named it Teotihuacán,

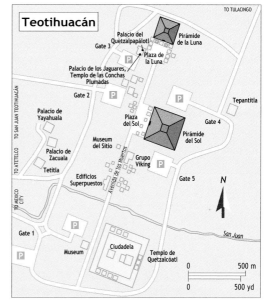

Teotihuacán

TO TULACINGO

Palacio del Quetzalpapálotl
Gate 3
Pirámide de la Luna
Plaza de la Luna
Palacio de los Jaguares, Templo de las Conchas Plumadas
Gate 2
TO SAN JUAN TEOTIHUACAN
Palacio de Yayahuala
Palacio de Zacuala
Museum del Sitio
Tetitla
Edificios Superpuestos
Gate 1
TO ATETELCO
TO MEXICO CITY
Plaza del Sol
Avenida de los Muertos
Grupo Viking
Pirámide del Sol
Gate 4
Tepantitla
Gate 5
N
San Juan
Museum
Ciudadela
Templo de Quetzalcóatl
0   500 m
0   500 yd

Above: *A massive stone staircase leads to the top of the Pyramid of the Sun at Teotihuacán.*

which means 'the place where the gods were born' (the city's original name is not known), and thought that the gods created the universe from here.

The city was arranged around the **Avenida de los Muertos**, a long, central thoroughfare which now serves as the main road for tourists and itinerant vendors. The less popular routes through the ruins afford a more tranquil course and time for contemplation.

Prime buildings include the **Pirámide del Sol**, the world's third largest pyramid at 70m (230ft) high, with a 248-step access to the spectacular views at the top; the beautifully proportioned **Pirámide de la Luna**, situated at the northern end of the axis; the nearby **Palacio del Quetzalpapálotl**; the **Palacio de los Jaguares**, with its jaguar murals; the **Templo de las Conchas Plumadas**, so called for the flower and feather decorations on its façade; and the **Ciudadela**, a large sunken plaza containing buildings such as the **Templo de Quetzalcóatl**, also known as the Pyramid of the Feathered Serpent, with its marvellous and well-preserved carvings. The site can be scorchingly hot, especially at midday, so a hat and bottle of water are essential.

FAVOURITE FRUITS

Ananas • pineapple
Mango • mango
Manzana • apple
Naranja • orange
Granadilla • passionfruit or grenadilla
Guanabana • a pear-like fruit
Guyaba • guava
Higo • fig
Limón • lime or lemon
Piña • pineapple
Plátano • banana

SOUTH OF MEXICO CITY

Easily accessible from the capital for a day tour (though meriting considerably longer), Cuernavaca is a weekend retreat for wealthy residents of Mexico City. Further south is the picture-postcard colonial town of Taxco.

Cuernavaca ★★

Cuernavaca has a delightful spring-like climate and a large population of foreigners and wealthy Mexicans, some of whom open their lavish properties to visitors.

Before 1519, Cuernavaca was home to the Tlahuicas, then the Aztecs (some claim Moctezuma was born here), and later to Hernán Cortés, who is accredited with introducing sugar cane to the region.

The *zócalo* – **Plaza de Armas** – provides the focal point of the city, along with the neighbouring **Jardín Juárez** (note the gazebo designed by Gustave Eiffel). Nearby, the Palacio de Cortés (which was indeed his home, built on pre-Hispanic remains) houses the **Museo de Cuauhnáhuac**, a tribute to Mexican history and culture. The impressive mural by Rivera recounts the history of the country from the arrival of the Spanish to the Revolution.

The superb **Jardín Borda**, created for silver magnate Joseph de la Borda, is part of a private estate which is now open to the public. While waiting for the completion of their own residence, Emperor Maximilian and Empress Carlotta stayed in a large mansion, part of which has been turned into the **Museo de la Herbolaría**, or Herb Museum, which alone is worth the journey to Cuernavaca. Another interesting museum, the **Museo Robert Brady**, was once the extensive private collection of Brady, a wealthy American resident.

Two festivals that make a trip to Cuernavaca even more memorable (book ahead for hotels) are **Carnaval** and **Día de la Virgen de Guadalupe**.

> ### BEHIND THE GATES
>
> Some of Cuernavaca's loveliest **mansions** and **homes** can be viewed as part of a specialized tour offered by the local Ladies' Guild. Details of these tours can be found in Sunday's travel supplement in the *Mexico City News*.

Below: *Part of the flat Valley of Mexico, one of the country's most populated regions.*

Opposite: *A private courtyard, with an ornate fountain, in Puebla.*
Below: *The hill-hugging colonial town of Taxco.*

Taxco **

A national historical monument, Taxco is not only Mexico's silver town *par excellence* but a gem of a colonial city. About halfway between Mexico City and Acapulco, the hill-hugging town of Taxco is undeniably picturesque, has a pleasant climate and is full of pretty plazas (not to mention silver shops).

The Aztecs had already discovered the silver and gold veins around Taxco, but it was Frenchman **Joseph de la Borda** who discovered a particularly rich lode and then financed some of the town's colonial buildings.

Taxco is a maze of twisting, cobbled streets and quaint whitewashed buildings but the centre is still the *zócalo*, **Plaza Borda,** with the impressive pale pink **Iglesia de Santa Prisca**, built by Borda, whose interior takes Baroque decoration to the extreme. Thanks to another foreigner, American William Spratling, Taxco's reputation as a place to buy silverware was established. His former **workshop** is open to the public. Today Taxco has hundreds of silver shops along with the small **Museo de la Plateria**. Other museums in the town include the **Museo Virreinal** (Casa Humboldt) which displays a collection of pre-Columbian items and religious art.

To see Taxco from the air and also to marvel at the surrounding mountain panorama, you take the **teleférico** from Los Arcos and then ascend to the luxurious Monte Taxco hotel.

Semana Santa is a great time to visit Taxco, but be sure to book your accommodation well in advance.

SOUTHEAST OF MEXICO CITY

To the southeast of Mexico City lie the two colonial cities of Puebla (famed for its brightly coloured tiles) and Tlaxcala. Archaeological highlights in the region include the stunning polychromatic murals at Cacaxtla.

Puebla ★★★

Located between Mexico City and the Caribbean port of Veracruz, Puebla was built on a hill so that the Spanish could keep an eye on trade. The Spanish settlers' predilection for adorning their homes and civic buildings with colourful brick and locally produced talavera ceramics makes for great photography, especially with a backdrop of the snow-capped volcanoes. Indeed, UNESCO designated Puebla a World Heritage Site in the hopes of conserving it.

The *zócalo*, or **Plaza Principal**, forms the heart of this city and is surrounded by several elegant arched walkways, sidewalk cafés and restaurants. Here is the beautiful **Catedral**, second largest in Mexico, with its two impressive bell towers. The **Iglesia de Santo Domingo**,

Puebla map

- Av. 18 Poniente
- ex-Convento de Santa Mónica ★
- Templo de Santa Mónica
- Av. 16 Poniente / Av. 14 Oriente
- Av. 14 Poniente
- ex-Convento de Santa Rosa ★
- Museo del Ferrocarril ★
- Av. 12 Poniente / Av. 12 Oriente
- Av. 10 Poniente / Av. 10 Oriente
- Av. 8 Poniente / Av. 8 Oriente
- Iglesia de San Francisco
- Av. 6 Poniente / Av. 6 Oriente
- Casa del Alfeñique ★
- Iglesia de Santo Domingo △
- El Parián / Crafts Market
- Av. 4 Poniente / Av. 4 Oriente
- Templo de Santa Catalina / Museo Universitario
- Talavera Uriarte ★
- Av. 2 Poniente / Av. 2 Oriente
- ROYALTY (H) △ ★ (H) PALACIO SAN LEONARDO
- Fonda Santa Clara
- Av. Reforma / Av. Juan de Palafox y Mendoza
- Paseo Bravo
- Zócalo / Iglesia de la Compañía
- Av. 3 Poniente / Av. 3 Oriente
- Museo Bello
- △ Catedral
- Av. 5 Poniente / Av. 5 Oriente
- i ★ Biblioteca Palafox
- Av. 7 Poniente / Av. 7 Oriente
- ★ Museo Amparo
- Av. 9 Poniente / Av. 9 Oriente
- Patio de ★ los Azulejos
- Av. 11 Poniente / Av. 11 Oriente
- Blvd Heroes del 5 de Mayo
- Calles: 11 Norte, 9 Norte, 7 Norte, 5 Norte, 3 Norte, Av. 5 de Mayo, 2 Norte, 4 Norte, 6 Norte
- Calles: 11 Sur, 9 Sur, 7 Sur, 5 Sur, 3 Sur, 16 de Septiembre, 2 Sur, 4 Sur, 8 Sur
- 0 400 m / 0 400 yd
- TO (H) CROWNE PLAZA

Right: *Originating in Spain, these beautiful Talavera ceramics are produced in Puebla.*
Opposite: *A unique Carnival celebration, rarely seen by tourists, takes place annually at Huejotzingo.*

MOLE POBLANO

It was from **Puebla** that *Mole Poblano* took its name. This blend of **spices**, a dose of **chocolate**, with a kick from **chillies**, comes in a variety of colours and flavours, and is served with turkey, chicken and enchiladas. Puebla is likewise known for its red, green and white *chiles en nogada*, a mixture of stuffed chillies with walnut sauce. Supermarkets now sell the basic mix in cartons – a great way of recreating a Mexican meal back home.

---

with its highly regarded and breathtakingly ornate **Capilla del Rosarío**, is situated just a few blocks away. There are over 60 churches in Puebla, many of which are astonishingly beautiful.

Museums abound. Don't miss the **Museo Amparo** (archaeological exhibits of immense value), **Museo Bello** (arts, antiques and Talavera tiles all crammed into a colonial house), the beautiful **Casa del Alfeñique** (an elegant colonial mansion with beautiful architecture) and the **Biblioteca Palafox** (an irreplaceable collection of books and maps).

Arts and crafts, especially **Talavera ceramics**, can be found all over town. **Uriarte** has been producing such handmade pottery for over 150 years and offers informative guided tours of their factory. The crafts market, **El Parián**, is good for a variety of inexpensive handicrafts.

Puebla also has a number of former convents which are worth visiting. It was in the **ex-Convento de Santa Rosa** that *Mole Poblano* is said to have been created, while the pretty **ex-Convento de Santa Mónica** offers, among other sights, instruments of self-flagellation and other religious artefacts.

Puebla is also a good jumping-off point for the many interesting points in the state – the national parks of the volcanoes **Popocatépetl** and **Iztaccíhuatl**, the small town of **Huejotzingo**, and particularly for **Cholula**.

Cholula ★

The most important sight in Cholula is the **Tepanapa Pyramid** which, prior to Cortés' assault, was believed to have been the biggest in the world (now recognized as the second biggest), and parts of it date back over 2500 years. The Spanish constructed **La Virgen de los Remedios** on the rubble, and this is the church so often seen in photos with a backdrop of the snow-capped Popocatépetl.

Huejotzingo ★

Just 20km (12 miles) north of Puebla, this otherwise quiet town is noted for its colourful and slightly wild **carnival** celebrations held each Shrove Tuesday. A feast for locals, only a few tourists ever witness this riotous annual event.

Tlaxcala ★

Some 30km (19 miles) north of Puebla, the colonial town of Tlaxcala is a pleasant place to visit for its calm atmosphere. The central *zócalo*, the spacious and tree-filled **Plaza de la Constitución**, is pure colonial with its **Palacio del Gobierno** (look out for the huge murals inside by Xochitiotzin) and other stately buildings. The **ex-Convento San Francisco** dates back to 1526 and has an impressive wooden ceiling that recalls Moorish work in Spain. The **Santuario de la Virgen de Ocotlán** is a spectacular example of frothy Churrigueresque architecture.

Cacaxtla ★

Recently discovered, the ruins of Cacaxtla, 19km (12 miles) southwest of Tlaxcala, have thrown light on some of the missing elements in Mexico's historic development. The vivid **frescoes**, painted on the walls of a series of buildings, are believed to date from the height of the Classical period. The mural known as 'The Battle' depicts a fierce battle between one group wearing jaguar skins and a second, feathers, and is a breathtaking piece of work.

THE VOLCANOES

A national park encloses two of Mexico's most famous volcanoes, the snow-capped peaks of **Popocatépetl** ('smoking mountain') and **Iztaccíhuatl** ('sleeping woman'), which take their names from an Aztec legend. The warrior Popocatépetl was in love with Iztaccíhuatl, the daughter of the emperor. When the false news of his death in battle reached her, she died of a broken heart. Popocatépetl laid out her body on the mountain range and lit an eternal torch nearby, from where he watches over her. 'Popo' and 'Izta' are popular destinations for climbers and hikers.

Mexico City at a Glance

BEST TIMES TO VISIT

Nov–Apr is the best time to visit but pollution is at its highest then. **Summer rains** bring humidity and some pollution relief. Winter day temperatures are around 20°C (68°C) but drop to as little as 7°C (45°F) at night. Day temperatures rise to 26° or 27°C (79° to 81°F) in Apr and May but drop at night. Mexico City is particularly festive over **Semana Santa**, Easter Week; **May Day** or **Labour Day**.

GETTING THERE

Aeropuerto International Benito Juárez is the main gateway to the country, tel: 57 829 002 for general information. **Aeroméxico**, the country's main international carrier, has direct flights to over 50 airports worldwide. For information, tel: 133-4000 or 01 800 021 40 00 (800 numbers are free) from Mexico City. **Mexicana** also serves some cities in the US. For information, tel: 01-800-502-2000. Alternatively, many US airlines offer attractive rates for travel via a US gateway.

Four major long-distance **bus stations** serve cities nationwide while the main railway station, **Buenavista**, has services to major cities.

GETTING AROUND

Be careful in crowded buses, the metro and underpasses. **Metro-Bus**, a new transport system, crosses town from south to north on Insurgentes Avenue. The efficient but crowded **metro** is easy to use with plenty of maps available. **Taxis** are plentiful but take them only from official taxi ranks (*sitios*) or through radio taxis. **Walking** is often best.

WHERE TO STAY

Mexico City
LUXURY

Camino Real, Mariano Escobedo 700, tel: (5) 203-2121, fax: 250-6897. Flagship of one of Mexico's best hotel groups.
Fiesta Americana, Mariano Escobedo 756, col Anzures, tel: (5) 2581-1500. Luxurious, best view of Chapultepec's castle.
Hotel Nikko, Campos Eliseos 204, tel: (5) 280-1111, fax: 280-9191. Modern luxury from this premiere Japanese hotel in a Polanco-based building.
María Isabel Sheraton, Paseo de la Reforma 325, tel: (5) 5242-5555, fax: 5207-0684. Huge luxury hotel with good views from the top floors.

MID-RANGE

Gran Hotel, 16 de Septiembre 82, tel: (5) 510-4040 fax: 512-6772. Department store turned smart hotel, art nouveau style.
Majestic, Madero 73, tel: (5) 521-8600, fax: 512-6262. Old world, Great *Zócalo* location.

BUDGET

Hotel Catedral, Calle Doneceles 95, tel: (5) 512-8581, fax: 512-4344. Well-run,

popular, in great location.
Hotel Marlowe, Independencia 17, tel: (5) 521-9540, fax: 518-6862. Near Bellas Artes, central. Renovated hotel, good restaurant. Excellent value.

Outside Mexico City
LUXURY

Las Mañanitas, Linares 107, Cuernavaca, tel: (73) 14-1466, fax: 18-3672. Historic suite hotel, furnished with antiques.
Hotel Crowne Plaza, Av Hermanos Serdán 141, Puebla, tel: (22) 48-6055, fax: 48-7344. Large prize-winning hotel.

MID-RANGE

Posada María Cristina, Leyva 20, Cuernavaca, tel: (73) 18-2981, fax: 12-9126. Colonial building, lovely gardens, pool.
Posada de la Misión, Avenida de los Plateros, tel: (762) 25519, fax: 22198. Hotel has murals by Juan O'Gorman.
Hotel Palacio San Leonardo, 2 Oriente 211, Puebla, tel: (22) 46-0555, fax: 42-1176. Central location in a colonial building.

BUDGET

Hotel Colonial, Juan Aragon y Leon 19, tel/fax: (73) 18-6414. Popular, clean but basic hotel, central.
Hotel Agua Escondida, Plaza Borda 4, Taxco, tel: (762) 21166. Comfortable, clean hotel, in town centre.

WHERE TO EAT

Street food is delicious but not always healthy. Restaurants like

Mexico City at a Glance

Sanborn's and VIPS are relatively inexpensive. Smart restaurants abound in large hotels (US$15 and up for a meal). Set menus are excellent value.

Mexico City

LUXURY

San Ángel Inn, Diego Rivera 50, San Ángel, tel: (5) 616-1402. Meeting place of Pancho Villa and Emiliano Zapata.
Los Girasoles, Tacuba 8/10A, tel: (5) 510-0630. Beautiful décor, good Mexican cuisine.
La Valentina, Masaryk 513, Polanco, tel: (5) 282-2656. Nouvelle Mexican cuisine.

MID-RANGE

Sanborn's Casa de los Azulejos, Madero 4, Alameda, tel: (5) 5512-2233. One of many Sanborn's but a great location.
Café de Tacuba, Tacuba 28, Centro Histórico, tel: (5) 512 8482. Opened 1912, old-world, immensely popular for lunch. Go early. Mexican cuisine.
De Lao Cantina, Copenhague 32, Zona Rosa, tel: (5) 207-3906. Trendy; unusual decorations by Bustamante.
Restaurante Terrazza, Hotel Majestic, Av Madero 73, tel: (5) 521-8600. Zócalo views and good Mexican cuisine.
Villa María, Homero 704, Polanco, tel: (5) 250-1841. Good haute cuisine, Mexican.

Outside Mexico City

MID-RANGE

Mesones Sacristía de la Compañía, Calle 6 Sur 304,

tel: (22) 42-3554. Trendy courtyard ambience.
El Resguardo de los Angeles, 6 sur 504, Puebla, tel: (22) 46-4106. Patio restaurant, Mexican and international cuisine.
La India Bonita, Morrow 15, Cuernavaca. Attractive restaurant. Good Mexican food.
Señor Costilla's, Plaza Borda, Taxco. Part of Carlos Anderson chain. Mexican, international.

BUDGET

Restaurant Santa Fe, Hidalgo 2, Taxco. Recommended by locals, Mexican food.

NIGHTLIFE

Travel after dark only in official taxis. The **Ballet Folklórico de México**, Palacio de Bellas Artes, tel: (5) 5529-9320, performs Wednesday and Sunday evenings, and Sunday afternoon. Booking essential.
Live Music at the Sheraton María Isabel bar Jorongo, tel: (5) 5242-5555.

SHOPPING

Zona Rosa, Polanco, hotel lobbies, department stores (El Nuevo Mundo, El Palacio de Hierro, Liverpool) and **markets**. **Mercado Insurgentes**, Metro Insurgentes; **Mercado de Artesanías San Juan**, Metro San

Juan; **Mercado La Ciudadela**, Metro Balderas; all open daily. **Exposición Nacional de Arte Popular**, Av Juárez 89, has excellent handicrafts from the country. **Centro Artesanal Buenavista** is a fixed-price store frequented by visitors.

Outside Mexico City, **Taxco** is a favourite stop for silver. There are said to be over 300 silver shops. Good selection in shops around Plaza Borda.

In **Puebla**, ceramics and onyx are tempting. **El Parián** crafts market has handicrafts.

USEFUL CONTACTS

British Consulate, Río Lerma 71, Cuauhtémoc, tel: (5) 207-2089.
US Consulate, Paseo de la Reforma 305, Cuauhtémoc, tel: (5) 5080-2000, 01 900 849849 (900 numbers are expensive). **Oficina de Turismo de la Ciudad de México** (tourist office), Amberes 54, Zona Rosa, tel: (5) 5208 1030.
Correo Mayor (GPO), Juan Ruiz de Alarcón; or in Zócalo area, Plaza de la Constitución 7. Open 08:00–20:00.
Aeroméxico, Paseo de la Reforma 80, tel: (5) 5133-4010.
Mexicana, Paseo de la Reforma 312, tel: (5) 5448-0990.

MEXICO CITY	J	F	M	A	M	J	J	A	S	O	N	D
AVERAGE TEMP. °F	68	73	77	81	82	77	75	73	72	72	70	68
AVERAGE TEMP. °C	20	23	25	27	28	25	24	23	22	22	21	20
RAINFALL in	1	1	1.5	2.5	3	4	6	5	4	2	2.5	1
RAINFALL mm	23	12	34	51	64	101	152	127	101	49	51	16

3
Baja California

Separated from Mexico's mainland by a long inlet of sea – the Gulf of California, also known as the Sea of Cortés – Baja California is rather different from the rest of the country. It came into existence some five million years ago when, due to some movement along the San Andreas Fault, it was torn apart from the rest of the land. Baja California today is a mountainous finger of desert, some 1250km (777 miles) long and 90km (56 miles) wide. Wild and untamed for the most part, it has unspoiled sandy beaches on either side.

Long before the Spanish set foot in Mexico, this land was inhabited by local cave-dwelling Indians. Cortés, ever on the lookout for riches, heard tales of bays filled with pearls, and organized an expedition to verify the story. As with other rumours in Mexico, the reality was somewhat different (and the Indians hostile), so it was not until 1697 that the Spanish decided to settle here. They began three Jesuit missions and set about converting the Indians. However, along with religion and agricultural practices, they also brought disease.

More recently, Baja California has become renowned as the place where migrating grey whales call in to mate, give birth to and nurse their young. This has, in turn, led to a substantial increase in tourism, especially from the southern United States. The most important development so far has taken place along the fabulous beaches between the small town of San José del Cabo and the now sprawlingly large Cabo San Lucas, a huge glitzy resort catering for the well-heeled.

DON'T MISS

*** **Grey whales:** around the Laguna Ojo de Liebre (Scammon's Lagoon) or at Bahía Magdalena.
** **Los Cabos:** visit Cabo San Lucas and San José del Cabo, and the fabulous beaches between these two resorts.
* **Sea of Cortés:** a wonderful array of flora and fauna for divers, snorkellers, kayakers.
* **Mulegé:** this is one of the prettiest towns on the shores of the Sea of Cortés.

Opposite: *The stark mountains of Baja meet the calm Mar de Cortés in a landscape of considerable beauty.*

CLIMATE

Most of Baja California has a **desert** climate, with searing summer temperatures that may reach 36°C (97°F), and little rainfall. **Winters** are warm and mild but can be chilly at night.

Opposite: *The Ensenada region has intensified its viticulture to earn its reputation as the country's premier wine-making area.*

TIJUANA

By far the busiest entry and exit point between the United States and Mexico, Tijuana is a border town (and Mexico's fourth largest city, with more than a million inhabitants) that is trying to lose its bad image. During **Prohibition** it thrived as a south-of-the-border drinking dive, including all the forms of entertainment that went with that. It is probably more American than Mexican, but it certainly attracts millions of visitors, many of whom come just for an afternoon or evening out, while others travel through here on their way south. It is also a major air hub for domestic services.

Tijuana thrives on shopping (especially in the area around **Avenida Revolución**), eating and entertainment. If you are travelling elsewhere in Mexico, these are probably not priorities. However, if you are in town during a Thursday **Jai Alai** ball game or a summer **Sunday bullfight**, then stop a while and join the fun.

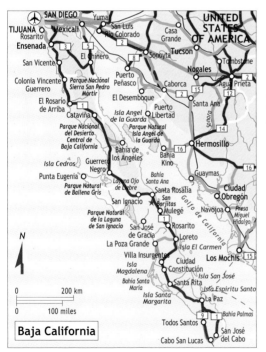

Baja California

MEXICALI

Another important border town and also the administrative capital of Baja California Norte, Mexicali (over half a million inhabitants) boasts the largest Chinese community, **La Chinesca**, in all of Mexico. Because of its alluvial soil, Mexicali is a prosperous agricultural town. Again, it is a city that is served by domestic airlines which connect with the capital.

Heading south from Tijuana (the best road here follows the western coastline), **Rosarito**, not so long ago just a fishing community, is the first beach resort you reach. In 1996 it was chosen for filming part of the movie *Titanic* and, as extras poured in and discovered its charms, it has remained a popular resort ever since.

ENSENADA

Baja's largest fishing port, Ensenada, has also developed into a tourist town and a temporary home for winter escapees from the United States. The beaches are like many others on the

peninsula, the deep-sea fishing is good, and the partying even better. Try some of its tasty seafood during your stay in town.

Further south, the foothills of the **San Pedro Martir** mountains are beautifully manicured by the vineyards which produce much of Mexico's better wines. Some of the wine estates here are open to visitors. To the east, the **Parque Nacional Sierra San Pedro Martir** is a rather interesting place to explore, for those who have their own vehicles. It has some high peaks, deep canyons and prolific coniferous forests.

El Rosario is a divide. It is the end of an easy weekend hop for Americans, and it is the place where the road turns east into the increasingly desert-like landscape, through *cardón* cacti and the unusual boojum trees, and up into the mountains toward **Cataviña**.

Bahía de Los Angeles ★

On a map there seems to be very little of interest to differentiate Bahía de Los Angeles but, protected by the large, uninhabited island of **Isla Angel de la Guarda** (Island of the Guardian Angel), Bahía de Los Angeles is nevertheless a wonderfully unspoiled detour from the main highway to a sandy beach, fine swimming and great fishing. Facilities are minimal but if the idea of swimming with dolphins and snorkelling around the shore appeals to you, this is a great find.

CALIFORNIAN WINES

In 1791, a Spanish missionary set up the St Thomas Aquinas Mission in what is now known as the **Valle de Santo Tomás**. From stocks brought by early settlers, sacramental wine was produced. After expropriation of church property in Mexico in the mid-1800s, the mission lands passed through various hands before two Ensenada pioneers bought the property in 1888 for wine making. The **Bodegas de Santo Tomás** is the second oldest winery in Baja California and was the first to produce wine commercially. It has reintroduced many vine stocks from Europe and, because of the favourable climate in the area, is able to produce a fine selection of wines at competitive prices. It offers a range of whites (Sauvignon Blanc, Chardonnay and Colombard) and reds (Cabernet Sauvignon, Merlot and Tempranillo). Visitors are welcome at their **Ensenada winery**.

GUERRERO NEGRO AND SURROUNDS

Named for the whaling vessel that broke up outside town in the mid-19th century, Guerrero Negro is the centre for **whale watching** and is also known for its production of **salt**, indeed producing some 30 per cent of the world's supply. The town holds no real interest for visitors other than as a place to stay while whale watching. Most travellers stay in one of the camps in the national park.

Above: *The telltale spout or flipping of a tail alerts the patient whale watcher to a nearby mammal.*
Opposite: *Bahía de la Concepción is a jewel of the Mar de Cortés.*

Traditionally, 5000-odd whales make the journey each January – nearly 10,000km (6214 miles) from the Bering Straits – and head for their familiar birthing waters in **Laguna Ojo de Liebre** and **Laguna Guerrero Negro** (they also go further south, to Laguna San Ignacio and Bahía Magdalena), returning north at the end of March.

The **Parque Natural de Ballena Gris** (Grey Whale Natural Park) in the Laguna Ojo de Liebre has been specifically set up to protect these gentle leviathans, and visitors to the park can sit on the shores and watch the activities of the whales through binoculars.

San Ignacio ★★

The dry and dusty road to Santa Rosalía passes through the town of San Ignacio, where a very fine mission church warrants a stop. This well-tended town is also the best jumping-off point for visiting some of the pre-Columbian cave paintings in the region.

Accessible from San Ignacio, the **Laguna San Ignacio** is at the centre of a big debate, as plans to expand the saltworks here are possible, bringing jobs to thousands of poorly employed Mexicans. The downside is that the environmentalists fear this huge industry will have a punitive effect on the whales, many of which are already seeking shelter elsewhere along the coast.

RESERVA DE LA BIOSPHERA EL VIZCAINO

Between (and including the area formed by) the offshore islands Isla San Benito and Isla Cedros and the mainland at Guerrero Negro lies one of the world's largest **nature reserves**. Not only is it prime territory for **whale watching**, but this rugged area is known for its sea lions, seals, elephant seals, the Cedros mule deer and a whole host of **unusual flora**. There is little in the way of creature comforts but for the keen naturalist it is a fabulous place in which to hike.

Santa Rosalía ★

If Baja is predominantly Mexican, Santa Rosalía has a distinct French flavour. Founded in 1885 as the headquarters of the nearby French-owned copper mines, the town was built with France in mind and the architecture has much in common with that of the old French colonies. The best place to stay, the **Hotel Francés**, is also a historic legacy of those boom times. **Iglesia Santa Barbara**, a prefabricated iron church, was designed by that eminent civil engineer, Alexandre Gustave Eiffel. It is also the best place to visit the caves of **San Borjitas**, with their ancient paintings. The journey requires a guide and four-wheel drive. Santa Rosalía is linked with the mainland by a twice-weekly ferry which takes around seven hours to cross.

Mulegé ★

Southbound, the next stop is the small subtropical village of Mulegé, a mission town founded by the Jesuits in 1705. The mission, on a hillside upriver, is open to the public. Lining the town's streets are old buildings and brilliant bougainvilleas, while along the river banks dense groves of palm trees flourish. One of Mulegé's principle attractions is its beaches. In its sheltered bay, kayaking and fishing are popular, while offshore it is great for diving.

Between Mulegé and Loreto the road loops around the rather impressive shores of the immense **Bahía de Concepción**, with its pretty sandy beaches.

SEA OF CORTÉS

A cornucopia of species inhabit the Sea of Cortés and its shores. Despite less than 25mm (1 in) of rainfall annually, over 570 species of **plants** thrive here. There are over 30 species of **reptiles**, including the 60cm (24in) *chuckwalla* **lizard** and a huge concentration of **tropical birds**. In the water, over 850 species have been identified including the **grey whale**, the hump-nosed and pilot whale, manta ray, a number of turtles and dolphins. In the shallows, a myriad colourful **tropical fish** delight snorkellers and scuba divers alike.

LORETO

This is the epitome of a small Mexican mission town:
a tree-shaded main plaza where elders sit around and
while the day away, cobbled streets in the old centre, a
malécon (seaside promenade), and a 300-year-old mission
church, the **Misión Nuestra Señora de Loreto**. With the
creation of a national park – the **Parque Marino Nacional
Bahía de Loreto**, protecting over 2000km² (772 sq miles)
of shore, islands and sea – Loreto has become even more
popular with watersports enthusiasts and those looking for
a quiet place to relax. Whales, dolphins and plenty of
waterbirds are frequently spotted from the *malécon*.

For those visitors interested in the missions, a journey
of about 40km (25 miles) along dirt roads through some
truly outstanding mountain scenery leads to the well-
preserved **Misión San Francisco Javier**, which was also
founded 300 years ago. The breathtaking, rugged desert
scenery alone merits making such a dusty journey.

The route between
Loreto and La Paz
reverts to the western
side of the peninsula,
then it dips down in
the direction of the
semi-enclosed **Bahía
Magdalena**, protected
by the island of the
same name. This is
again prime whale-
watching territory
(*see* page 54) and it
is possible to view
these creatures from
the shores at Puerto
López Mateos, or else
from panga boats in
Puerto San Carlos,
which take visitors
out into the bay to
watch the whales.

LA PAZ

Situated in a deep, sheltered bay, La Paz is not only the major port on the Sea of Cortés but also one of its prime tourist resorts, due mainly to its pleasant atmosphere and world-class sportfishing. Fish such as tuna, sailfish, marlin and yellowtail are the prizes.

The Spanish landed in 1535 and found a number of hostile Indian tribes. They were not able to establish a mission here until the early 19th century, by which time many of the indigenous Indians had succumbed to the deathly illnesses the Europeans had brought. Black pearls were the magnet for Europeans, but these were also wiped out by disease and over-culling. In 1974 La Paz became the capital of Baja California Sur.

The town's long **malécon** is probably its most attractive part, while some of the newer streets sprawl back quite a long way from the waterfront. See the waterfront from the *malécon* around sunset, and then head a block into town and visit some of its good seafood restaurants.

There are several small museums worth seeing, if time permits. The **Museo Regional de Antropología y Historia** gives an insight into the history and development of Baja, the **Museo Comunitario de la Ballena** documents the whales, and the quirky **Museo de la Caricatura y Crítica Gráfica** looks at Mexican political satire.

La Paz' best beaches are to be found at **Balandra**, **Coyote** and **Tecolete**, while divers and nature lovers head for the **Isla Espíritu Santo**, just offshore.

Left: *Scuba diving excursions, to see the area's colourful corals and fish, are popular from La Paz.* **Opposite:** *Towering over the surrounding palm trees is the impressive mission at San Ignacio.*

WATERSPORTS

La Paz is known to many as one of the best places for watersports on the Sea of Cortés. The white, sandy shoreline around **Espíritu Santo Island** is much favoured for **kayaking**. Resident dolphin pods, whale sharks and sea lion colonies beckon **naturalists**, while **scuba divers** and **snorkellers** head out for the islands of **Las Ánimas**, **San José** or **Cerralvo** where, among the pelagics, hammerhead sharks, manta rays and groupers can usually be found. In addition, **sports fishermen** haul in huge catches in the warmer summer months.

LOS CABOS

The most fashionable place in Baja California to visit, the towns of Cabo San Lucas and San José del Cabo are collectively known as Los Cabos. They are separated by 32km (20 miles) of road known as the 'Corridor', a route bordering some gorgeous beaches but one which is being developed into a burgeoning resort area, complete with world-class sportfishing and six championship golf courses.

San José del Cabo ★★

Coming along the eastern coast from La Paz, San José del Cabo is the first of the two towns you will encounter. With just over 20,000 inhabitants, it is quite small and has managed to retain a certain degree of its typical Mexican atmosphere. It has a shady, central square – the **Plaza Mijares** – and narrow streets; also fashionable **Boulevard Mijares** with its restaurants and souvenir shops, some attractive Spanish-influenced architecture and, nearby, a number of beautiful beaches.

Just a couple of kilometres away the **Estero de San José**, now a nature reserve, protects over 200 species of bird that migrate annually to and from the Río San José. There are pleasant walkways here, from which visitors can view the waterbirds.

The drive to the south between San José del Cabo and Cabo San Lucas used to be a tranquil one with great sea views. However, the traffic now counts earth-moving equipment, busy relandscaping the scenery into perfect golf courses, beautiful holiday homes and expensive modern hotels. In between, a few side tracks lead to the glorious beaches where snorkelling and swimming are still good and, better yet, free.

LOS CABOS SHOPPING

Besides **handicrafts** from the mainland, and local Baja California Sur **works of art**, look out for **interior design** in the Los Cabos area. Because of its wealthy American clientele, Los Cabos has built up a reputation for interesting and innovative fabrics, furniture and decorative items for the smart home. It is certainly a place to stock up on merchandise (and ideas). Shops are able to ship goods worldwide. Check out **El Callejón**, **Decoramerica**, **Galería El Dorado** and **Galerías Gattamelata** in Cabo San Lucas, or **Galería de Los Cabos**, **ADD**, **Copal Galería** and **Galería Sunshine** in San José.

Cabo San Lucas ★★

One of the country's prime resorts, the town of Cabo San Lucas (with 24,000 inhabitants) has developed out of recognition over the past five years. Its small fishing community has been swamped by commercial fishing, the new **Marina Cabo San Lucas** and its flotilla of yachts, 24-hour partying, and serious shopping.

There are numerous water-borne trips that depart from Cabo San Lucas. The arch, which features in so many photographs, is a prime destination, while **scuba divers** and **snorkellers** generally head for the Roca Pelícano sea lion colony and the reef off **Chileno**, which is located approximately 14km (9 miles) east of town. Beach-lovers prefer the **Playa Médano** on the Bahía de Cabo San Lucas, the more distant **Playa del Amor** with its colonies of gulls and pelicans and, down the Corridor, **Playa Santa María** and **Playa Chileno**. Other options include renting **kayaks** and exploring the coves and, of course, **game fishing**. The best fishing season is in October and November when annual tournaments pack in the crowds. Lastly, though for many people the only reason to visit Los Cabos, there is **golf**. The fees are rather high, but the courses are wonderful.

After sports and before partying, the local shops are worth a visit. Mexican folk art, pottery and hammocks are among the good buys. **El Rancho** and **Galería Dorado** in particular have good quality items.

After dark, the volume increases dramatically, and the numerous bars, restaurants and discos really get into top gear. The choice of venues is vast and the menus are as international as the clientele.

TODOS SANTOS

One interesting excursion from Los Cabos is to head northwards along the beautiful western shores of Baja to **Todos Santos**. All Saints, as it translates, was just a small farming community near spectacular Pacific beaches, in the middle of nowhere, when a few **artists** and shrewd **foreigners** were drawn to it and settled, one by one, forming an interesting community of folk keen on keeping the environment **natural**. Many of the old adobe homes have been **renovated** and some of these now house excellent **restaurants** and **cafés**. Todos Santos has also developed a name for its **organic farming techniques**, and produce now finds its way onto the tables of Los Cabos.

Opposite: *The marina at Cabo San Lucas. This fashionable resort town is renowned mainly for its sport fishing and also for its excellent beaches.*

Baja California at a Glance

BEST TIMES TO VISIT

Any time of year is good. Hot in summer, Baja California is cooler in winter but as it has a desert-like climate in parts, annual rainfall is minimal.

GETTING THERE

Many tourists fly to California and take Greyhound buses or taxis to the border. If you are travelling south by **private vehicle**, border crossings can be slow and complex. **Buses** run from Tijuana to La Paz (24 hours), stopping en route at Guerrero Negro (12 hours) and Loreto (18 hours). Regular **flights** on Aero California, Aeroméxico and Mexicana (or Aerolitoral) connect Tijuana, La Paz, San José del Cabo and Loreto with the mainland. **Ferries** link the mainland with La Paz (twice weekly) and Santa Rosalia (six times weekly to Los Mochis and Mazatlán).

GETTING AROUND

Baja bus services with Elite and Crucero are frequent and good. Car rentals are popular and best prepaid in your home country. Major **car rental** companies are present in Tijuana, Los Cabos and La Paz.

WHERE TO STAY

Hotels are less sophisticated – except in Los Cabos – than elsewhere in Mexico as the majority of travellers arrive in their own recreational vehicles and use campsites.

LUXURY

Camino Real Tijuana Paseo de los Héroes, Tijuana, tel: (66) 33-4000, fax: 33-4001. A modern hotel in the better part of town.
Crowne Plaza, Blvd López Mateos and Av de los Héroes, Mexicali, tel: (65) 57-3600, fax: 57-0555. Very central.
Posada de las Flores, Fco Madero, Esq. Salvatierra, Loreto, tel: (113) 51162. Delightful, central, small hotel in renovated building full of antiques. Italian restaurant.
Crowne Plaza, Marina Norte Fidepaz, La Paz, tel: (112) 22744, fax: 40837. New hotel, good facilities, in a quiet area out of town centre.
Las Ventanas al Paraíso, Cabo Real, tel: (114) 40300, fax: 40255. Exquisite luxury, stunning views.
Hotel Palmilla, Highway 1, Km 27.5, south of San José, tel: (114) 20582, fax: 21706. Beautiful luxurious hotel in prime setting, decorated with Mexican art. Sea facing. Outstanding golf course.
Meliá Cabo Real Beach and Golf Resort, Highway 1, Km 19.5, south of San José, tel: (114) 40000, fax: 40101. Great golf courses.

MID-RANGE

Holiday Inn Vita Spa Agua Caliente, Paseo de los Héroes 18818, Tijuana, tel: (66) 34-6901, fax: 34-6912. Situated in the smarter part of town with a much-appreciated spa.

La Lucerna, Av Benito Juárez 2151, Mexicali, tel: (65) 64-7000, fax: 66-4706. Popular hotel, slightly out of town.
Oasis Hotel, Calle de la Playa, Loreto, tel: (113) 50112, fax: 50795. Beachfront hotel with bungalows. Fine tropical gardens full of birds.
Los Arcos and **Las Cabañas de Los Arcos**, Paseo Obregón, La Paz, tel: (112) 22744, fax: 54313. Beachfront hotel with newer bungalows. Good restaurants and sports facilities.
La Playita, Pueblo la Playa, San José, tel and fax: (114) 24166. Delightful, small friendly hotel on beach. Good restaurant.
Fiesta Inn, Blvd Malecón, San José, tel: (114) 20793, fax: 20480. Beachside, garden hotel with good amenities.
The Bungalows, Calle Libertad & Av Cabo San Lucas, Cabo San Lucas, tel: (114) 30585, fax: 35035. Small, gourmet B&B hotel in residential area. Rooms with kitchenettes.

BUDGET

Hotel Posada San Martín, Juárez 4, Loreto, tel: (113) 50442. Near both beach and Plaza Cívica. Simple, clean, very popular and excellent value.
Pensión California, Degollado 209, La Paz, tel: (112) 22896. Small, clean, popular and very inexpensive.
Bobo's Burro Inn, Libertad (near Abasolo) s/n, Cabo San Lucas. Ultrasimple accommo-

dation, clean and central.

LUXURY

La Embotelladora Vieja, Av Miramar 666, Ensenada, tel: (61) 74-0807. Excellent restaurant, good seafood and wines.
El Nido, Calle Salvatierra 154, Loreto, tel: (113) 50284. Amero-Mexican, steak and seafood. Moderate to expensive.
Damiana's, Blvd Mijares, San José, tel: (114) 20499. Great ambience, good seafood.
La República, Morelos Esq. 20 de Noviembre, Cabo San Lucas, tel: (114) 33400. Serves modern Mexican cuisine in a pretty setting.

MID-RANGE

Sanborn's, Revolución & Calle 8a, Tijuana. Mexican and International dishes.
Bougainvillea, Malecón de Vista Coral, La Paz, tel: (1) 22-7744. Elegant, international and seafood cuisine, with attracive ambience.
Zipper's, Costa Azul, Corridor. Beachfront café, great views. Mexican and international.
Pancho's, Hidalgo, Cabo San Lucas, tel: (114) 30973. Noisy, fun, Mexican food.

BUDGET

Hugo's Mi Oficina, Benito Juárez & Mijares, San José. Modest ambience, excellent seafood and Mexican cuisine.
Tropicana Bar & Grill, Blvd. Mijares 30, San José, tel: (114) 22311. Centrally located and renowned for its good food and pleasant atmosphere.

Tijuana pulsates with nightlife. Av Revolución is the busiest with places like **Hard Rock Café**; Zona Río is more upmarket. Midnight rodeos at **Rodeo la Media Noche**. **Cabo San Lucas** is party town. **Planet Hollywood**, **Cabo Wabo Bar & Grill** and **Hard Rock Café** are always packed.

Los Cabos has a good selection of furnishings (*see* box, page 58). Cabo San Lucas' **Mercado Mexicano** is a good place to search for folk art. **J&J Habanos** (three locations in Cabo San Lucas) is thé place for cigars.
La Paz has an interesting selection of Baja California art at **Paisajes Sudcalifornia**.

US Consulate, Boulevard Marina, Cabo San Lucas, tel: (114) 33566.
Semantur ferry services, freephone tel: 01-800-696-9600.
Tourist Offices
Loreto: Plaza Cívica, tel: (113) 50036.
La Paz: Mariano Abasolo, tel: (112) 40424.

Cabo San Lucas: Fondo Mixto de Promoción Turística, Madero, tel: (114) 21566.
San José del Cabo: Zaragoza, tel: (114) 21566.
Airlines
Aeroméxico: freephone tel: 01-800- 021-4000.
Los Cabos: Blvd Lazaro Cardenas, Cabo San Lucas and at the airport, tel: (114) 20397.
La Paz: Paseo Obregón, tel: (112) 46366.
Mexicana, freephone tel: 01-800-849-1529.
Los Cabos: Paseo Los Cabos, Plaza Los Cabos, tel: (114) 20230.
Aero California
La Paz: Paseo Obregón, tel: (112) 51023.
Los Cabos: airport, tel: (114) 33700.
Sports contacts
Cabo Acuadeportes, tel and fax: (114) 30117. Scuba diving, snorkelling and kayaking.
Solmar Sport Fishing Fleet, tel: (114) 30646, fax: 30410.
Golf Courses in Los Cabos
Cabo del Sol, tel: (114) 58200, fax: 58202.
Cabo Real Golf Club, tel: (114) 40040.
Cabo San Lucas, tel: (114) 34653.
Palmilla Golf Club, tel and fax: (114) 45250.

LOS CABOS	J	F	M	A	M	J	J	A	S	O	N	D
AVERAGE TEMP. °F	73	74	77	81	86	88	91	90	88	86	81	75
AVERAGE TEMP. °C	23	23	25	27	30	31	33	32	31	30	27	24
RAINFALL in	–	0.5	–	–	–	–	0.5	1	10	–	1	1
RAINFALL mm	–	12	–	–	–	–	13	29	250	–	13	12

4
Northern Mexico

North of **Zacatecas** the country takes on a different aspect. This is no longer tourist Mexico, nor a country influenced much by colonialism, but a wild, harsh, yet starkly beautiful land where life is fashioned by the terrain and the climate. The winds cut to the bone in winter and the sun shows no mercy to man or beast in summer. The rugged Sierra Madre mountains, scored by deep ravines and dusty desert panoramas with the occasional cacti or spiky aloe, characterize Mexico's frontier territory.

The central highlands lured the Spanish with rumours of cities built of gold, but they found none. They did, however, find hefty veins of gold, silver and copper, and also some shy tribes, the most famous of which are the **Tarahumara**, in the Copper Canyon region.

Today's visitors hasten southwards, enticed by the makings of man, missing as they travel what others describe as the 'real Mexico': timeless villages, magnificent scenery and modern metropolises like **Monterrey** where, through both hard work and hard play, a new Mexican culture is being established.

The frontier towns – **Matamoros**, **Nuevo Laredo** and **Ciudad Juárez** – have their own identities culled from both sides of the border. Raucous, crowded, throbbing with neon and lacking in charm, they are not places to linger.

The most popular part to explore in this vast area is the famous Barranca del Cobre, the **Copper Canyon** – an enormous series of canyons through which a railway, the Chihuahua al Pacífico, drops from the *altiplano* down to Los Mochis on the Gulf of California.

TOP ATTRACTIONS

*** Chihuahua al Pacífico: follow the railway line running through the spectacular Copper Canyon from Chihuahua to Los Mochis, or vice versa.
** Chihuahua: a wealthy colonial town and home to various famous Mexican revolutionaries.
* Monterrey: this modern metropolis epitomizes northern Mexico's culture and industry.
* Northern Sonora: unspoilt and secluded beaches.

Opposite: *Late afternoon in the colourful Barranca del Cobre, also known as the Copper Canyon.*

Summer temperatures in Sonora and the border towns can be scorchingly hot, and **November** to **April** are generally the best and the coolest months to visit northern Mexico. However, winter nights in the Copper Canyon can drop to near freezing and it may even snow.

Opposite: *Northern Mexico is cowboy country and is the best place to buy boots, hats and horse tack.*

DURANGO

To the north of Zacatecas, the road splits into Routes 49 and 40. Route 40 turns in a northwesterly direction, heading for the town of Durango. The Spanish followed this very same route over 400 years ago, urged onward by rumours of riches. What glittered, however, was in fact not gold but iron ore (although the hills in this region do have veins of precious metals in them). Undeterred, the Spanish settled in 1563 at the foot of the **Cerro de Mercado** and founded Durango. A town of approximately 500,000 today, it owes its wealth to the exploitation of iron ore.

In the heart of town is the **Plaza de Armas** with, on its northern side, the large **cathedral**. The **Palacio del Gobierno** houses the local tourist office. Outside town, Durango owes its fame to quite another industry: the movies. In the small towns of **Chupadero** and **Villa del Oeste** a number of westerns, including *Big Jake* starring John Wayne, were filmed.

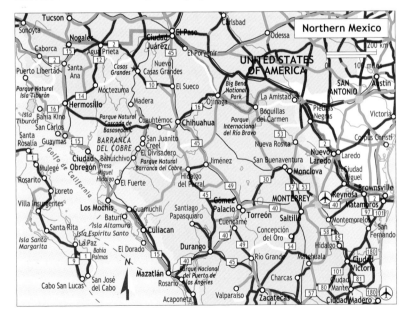

MONTERREY

Towering over the façade of Monterrey's cathedral is its monument to success: the **Lighthouse of Commerce**. The juxtaposition of old and new characterizes much of this city. Founded in 1596, Monterrey is one of Mexico's most prosperous cities, thanks to its large brewery and the reserves of natural gas in the region. Worth visiting are the Lighthouse of Commerce, the **Palacio del Gobierno** and **El Obispado** – the Bishop's Palace.

CHIHUAHUA

Silver put Chihuahua on the map. The sierras here bear huge lodes of silver, and the city, founded in 1709 after the metal was discovered here, is still Mexico's leading producer of silver. Cattle added to its wealth and today this large state (its surface area could cover 70 per cent of Spain) is said to produce Mexico's best beef. Chihuahua counts itself among the more affluent cities in the country.

A number of colourful personalities have lived in the city. The uprising that led to the Mexican Revolution in 1910 took form here under Pancho Villa and Francisco Madero. Father Miguel Hidalgo, father of the revolution, was executed here in 1811 and his body buried in the **Iglesia de San Francisco**. Revolutionaries Ignacio Allende and Juan Aldama also faced the firing squad in Chihuahua.

In the centre of the old town is the ornate **Catedral**, a fine Colonial-style building begun in 1717 but, because of Indian uprisings, taking over a century to complete. The **Palacio del Gobierno** (housing the tourist office) was the site of many an execution, while the **Museo Nacional de Chihuahua** offers a selection of interesting artefacts from Casas Grandes as well as displays on the life and customs of the large **Mennonite community** who have lived in Los Llanos, near Chihuahua, for some 80 years.

Quinta Luz, once the home of Pancho Villa, is now the **Museo de la Revolución** where Villa's official widow (he was reputed to have fathered offspring with more than 26 other women!) remained until her death in 1984.

FROM BEER TO STEEL

Dos Equis, one of Mexico's favourite beers, is brewed at **Cuauhtémoc-Moctezuma brewery** in **Monterrey**. This highly successful brewery has today diversified even further out of need to provide components for its beer. It began with **glass bottles** and then **metal caps**. It is now a world leader in the manufacture of glassware (producing not just bottles but also car windows and even fine crystal) and of ultrathin steel sheets.

Right: *Two daily departures, in both directions, take passengers on a sinuous and breathtaking day-long train journey through the Copper Canyon.*
Opposite: *Tropical El Fuerte is a welcome sight to visitors arriving on the train from sometimes-chilly Chihuahua.*

PRECIOUS PETS

Chihuahuas, those small hairless dogs, now a highly prized and rather expensive domestic **pet**, originated from the city of the same name. They were originally considered **pests**, until a fad was created for these rather unfortunate-looking dogs and their future was assured.

Barranca del Cobre (The Copper Canyon) ★★★

Statistics abound about this fabulous series of canyons in the midst of the Sierra Madre Occidental. Simply, it is one of the most impressive natural phenomena in Mexico. The best way to see it is from the slow-moving Chihuahua al Pacífico railway which winds its way from Chihuahua to Los Mochis (or vice versa) through the Sierra homeland of the fleetfooted Tarahumara Indians, a pastoral tribe who have resisted influences from the outside world and still live in rudimentary communities.

From north to south (the journey can also be done in reverse) the first stop is **Cuauhtémoc**, a large Mennonite community. Four hours later, amid pine-forested ravines, the train pulls into **San Juanito**, the centre of a logging industry. The smell of pine fills the air. Other industries, less legitimate, also exist in this area, and visitors are advised to ramble only if accompanied by reputable guides.

Most visitors alight at **Creel** where there is a range of accommodation, plenty of excursions and the chance to hike the impressive Tarahumara territory. Further down the line, **El Divisidero** (with the most spectacular view of the canyon) and **Bahuichivo** are both good spots to stop over. It is a long journey (the train is often late) to **El Fuerte**, once the capital of northwest Mexico. Many passengers alight at this delightful colonial town (*see box, opposite page*). The train pulls into **Los Mochis** (on the Gulf of California) at night, four climatic zones later.

Northern Sonora

Hardly the very first place that springs to mind when mentioning resorts, northern Sonora is, however, grossly underrated. Inland it is arid and mountainous, deathly hot in summer, and bone-shakingly cold in winter. But the **beaches** and swimming are good, there is wildlife in the hinterland, and the inland mountains hide a number of interesting sights such as the **Selva Encantada** (a forest of cacti) and some ancient rock paintings.

The capital of the state, **Hermosillo**, is 100km (62 miles) inland in a fertile valley. Its name means 'little beauty', but it doesn't live up to its translation. Most visitors move on.

The principal port of Sonora, **Guaymas**, thrives on its fishing industry. Its **Iglesia de San Fernando** was built by the Jesuits in the mid-18th century when they founded a mission here. There are regular **ferries** across the Sea of Cortés to Santa Rosalía, Baja California.

Just over 20km (12 miles) north of Guaymas, where the desert joins the shore, lie **Bacochibampo** and **San Carlos**, which have developed into the state's most popular resort complexes. With the endorsement of Club Méditerranée and other upmarket hotels, tourists flock here.

Further south and inland from the coast lies **El Fuerte,** near the **Presa Miguel Hidalgo** (Mexico's pre-miere bass fishing waters) while still further south is **Los Mochis**, known to most travellers as the starting or finishing point for the Chihuahua al Pacífico railway.

Chihuahua al Pacífico

The Chihuahua al Pacífico train takes 12 hours to travel the 672km (418 miles) between **Chihuahua** and **Los Mochis**, though it frequently runs late. The train runs over 39 bridges, goes through 86 tunnels and rises from sea level to the 2700m (8859ft) *altiplano*. Two daily trains travel in both directions: one, destined for the **local Tarahumara**, which starts at 07:00 and stops over 50 times along the route, and the **tourist train** which heads out at 06:00, makes seven selected stops and permits tourists to alight briefly at each stop for photos and snacks, or even to overnight in one of the hotels (the better to explore the magnificent scenery and local settle-ments). Smart travellers opt to get on (or off) the train at **El Fuerte**, a pretty colonial town in the tropical lowlands, which cuts at least an hour off the long journey and provides a more attractive destination than the town of Los Mochis.

BORDER TOWNS

For many, **Matamoros**, **Nuevo Laredo** and **Reynosa** are the entry points from the USA to Mexico. Despite efforts by local governments to give these towns a better image, they remain exactly what they always were: border crossing points where entertainment is far from refined, bars are crowded and rowdy, and shops abound with popular Mexican trinkets.

Matamoros has a rather better image than the other border towns, and manages to give over-the-border shoppers a taste of Mexico in a fairly clean environment. However, if you are travelling south, fill up with water and provisions, and head on down from here.

Further west, where the Río Bravo del Norte turns north towards Colorado, **Ciudad Juárez**, Mexico's fifth largest city, is yet another bustling border town. Although it offers little to detain the traveller, it is worth noting that many domestic flights leave from this airport, and travellers often find it is more advantageous to buy domestic air tickets here rather than either in the USA or in Europe.

If you have time on your hands, a trip to the archaeological dig at **Casas Grandes** is worth the effort, for it is an important pre-Columbian site with remains of Toltec and Aztec buildings.

BORDER FACTS

Immigration records show that over 62 million **people** cross the border legally each year, from Ciudad Juárez to El Paso, while some 40,000 **vehicles** pass the frontier each day. In Nuevo Laredo, 27 million crossings are recorded annually, while nearby, in Matamoros, 23 million crossings are recorded each year. Most of these crossings are made by people **working** in the neighbouring country. Crossings not recorded are believed to run into the hundreds of thousands.

Right: *Tarahumara Indians are among the few original peoples still living in Mexico as they did when the conquistadors arrived.*

Northern Mexico at a Glance

Nov to **Apr** are the coolest months, **Oct** and **Nov** the greenest. On winter nights in the Copper Canyon the temperature can drop to near freezing and it can even snow, occasionally.

All the border towns have airports. From Mexico City there are direct, long-distance buses, in all categories. Travel between Los Mochis and Chihuahua is on the Chihuahua al Pacífico railway. Book ahead.

Buses run around all major towns. However, **walking** in the city centres is probably the easiest and most practical. The Chihuahua al Pacífico **railway** also serves dozens of small stops along its way.

There are plenty of hotels and motels in the area; rates are not calculated by the night, but by the hour.

LUXURY
Fiesta Inn, Blvd Ortiz Mena 2801, Chihuahua, tel: (14) 29-0100. This modern business hotel is located slightly out of centre.
Club Méditerranée Sonora Bay, Playa de los Algodones, Guaymas, tel: (622) 70007. Reservations from any Club Med office worldwide.

MID-RANGE
Hotel San Francisco, Victoria 409, Chihuahua, tel: (614) 439 9000. Central, relatively smart.
The Lodge at Creel (Best Western), López Mateos 61, Creel, tel: (145) 60071, fax: 60082. Comfortable wooden cabins, good restaurant, full excursions.
Mansíon Tarahumara (El Castillo), Divisadero, tel: (14) 15-4721, fax: 16-5444. Prices include meals and a tour.
Posada Del Hidalgo, El Fuerte, tel and fax: (689) 30242. Colonial building turned hotel.
Hotel Santa Anita, Leyva and Hidalgo, Los Mochis, tel: (68) 20046, fax: 12-0046. Popular with those doing the Barranca del Cobre Canyon: they make bookings for Canyon hotels.

BUDGET
Hotel Apolo, Juárez 907, Chihuahua, tel: (14) 16-1101. Central, basic but clean.
Rancho de Lencho, near Divisadero. Inexpensive, homestay.
Hotel Margarita's, Calle Chapultepec, Creel, tel and fax: (145) 60245. Friendly hotel.

MID-RANGE
La Calesa Chihuahuense, Juárez & Colon 3300, Chihuahua. Excellent steaks.

Nogales Restaurant and Bar El Cid, Obrégon 124, Nogales. Mexican and international menus.

BUDGET
Restaurant Caballo Bayo, Creel. Good steaks and Mexican meals.

Chihuahua is the place to buy hats, belts and cowboy boots. In the Copper Canyon, the Tarahumara Indians sell many handicrafts. The **Casa de las Artesianas y Museo**, Av Ferrocarril 178, is a good showcase for their work.

Tours and regular tickets for the **Chihuahua al Pacífico** train can be arranged through Hotel Santa Anita (see Where to Stay). Alternatively, Travel Agency Rojo y Casavantes runs private tours; Vicente Guerrrero 1207, tel: 415 5858, fax: 415 5384.

US Consulates
Ciudad Juárez: López Mateos Nte 924, tel: (16) 11-3000.
Matamoros: Calle 1 no. 232, tel: (88) 12-4402.
Nuevo Laredo: Allende 3330, tel: (87) 14-0512.

CHIHUAHUA	J	F	M	A	M	J	J	A	S	O	N	D
AVERAGE TEMP. °F	64	68	77	82	90	93	91	88	84	79	70	64
AVERAGE TEMP. °C	18	20	25	28	32	34	33	31	29	26	21	18
RAINFALL in	1	1	–	0.5	1	2	3.5	3.7	3.5	1.5	1	0.5
RAINFALL mm	29	25	–	13	32	44	79	84	77	36	28	12

5
Central Highlands

It was in the mountains around Mexico City that the Spanish first began to settle. In 1521 Charles V, the King of Spain, ordered the conquistadors to explore the new territory and to establish towns there. For approximately 300 years the Spanish colonized Mexico, labouring very hard to create towns reflecting what they had left behind in Spain. The region's wealthy silver mines enabled the colonists to bequeath amongst other legacies a glorious architectural gift. For many a traveller to the country, this is the essence of Mexico: graceful homes and haciendas, ornate Baroque churches, beautifully tiled patios, shady courtyards filled with a profusion of flowers, exuberant fiestas and a historical legacy that weaves the past and the present into a wonderfully rich tapestry.

Mexico has recognized the importance, both historic and economic, of these towns and has acted accordingly: it has embarked on conservation programmes, opened museums and renovated some of the more important churches. The towns of **San Miguel de Allende** and **Guanajuato** have been declared World Heritage Sites by UNESCO, while many people consider that **Zacatecas** ought to have the same honour. **Guadalajara**, which is the country's second largest city, is a marvellous historical showcase and as Mexican as they come, while **Pátzcuaro** is a delightful colonial town that still maintains its Indian heritage. The year-round mild, sunny climate in this region is even more of a reason for a visit to central Mexico.

DON'T MISS

*** Guadalajara: colonial city and Mariachi capital.
*** San Miguel de Allende: fashionable town for foreign residents; abundant arts and crafts are found here.
** Morelia: pay a visit to this beautiful colonial town.
** Pátzcuaro: a small Purépecha town with fabulous handicrafts.
** Zacatecas: silver-mining town with superb cathedral.
* Janitzio: small island with spectacular All Souls' Day celebrations in the heart of Purépecha land.

Opposite: *Thanks to silver, Zacatecas was able to create this cathedral.*

Above: *The Fuente Tarasca, in Morelia, commemorates the stoic Tarascan women.*
Opposite: *On the first of November each year, Mexico celebrates her dead with a colourful festival which is at its most authentic in Janitzio.*

MORELIA

Located in the Michoacán Highlands, Morelia was founded in 1541. Originally called Valladolid after the conquistadors' home town, its name was changed in honour of José María Morelos, a hero in the War of Independence. Local laws not only ensure the conservation of historic buildings but oblige the construction of new ones in a similar style. With the local dusky pink stone characterizing many of the colonial buildings, the result is delightful.

The heart of Purépecha country, Morelia is a seat of learning and culture. Its San Nicolás **university** is the oldest in the Americas, the Baroque **cathedral** is a magnificent accomplishment, and its museums (especially the **Museo Regional Michoacano**) put the region in perspective. All the major sights are within walking distance of the huge main *zócalo*, known either as **Plaza de Armas** or **Plaza de los Mártires** (for the various freedom fighters murdered here). In the centre, too, is the impressive **aqueduct** and an ancient pedestrian street, **Calzada Fray Antonio**, lined with trees and colonial homes. The pretty **Jardín de las Rosas** is a perfect place to relax over a cup of coffee.

CLIMATE

The climate in the central highlands is generally **temperate** year-round. Night temperatures are cool in most of the region's cities, but the days are agreeably warm and it rarely gets unbearably hot, even during the height of summer.

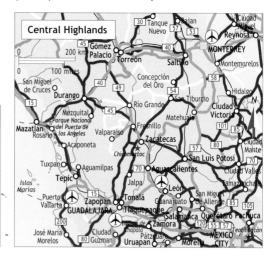

Morelia is a centre for buying folk art. The region produces a diverse selection of brass, candies (sweet-toothed travellers should head for the **Mercado de Dulces** for the ultimate treat), textiles, embroidery, guitars, and lacquerware. Look, then buy, at the **Casa de las Artesanías**.

The city is also a good point for exploring Michoacán and for visiting the **Sanctuario de Mariposas**, a reserve at El Rosario dedicated to the migratory Monarch butterfly.

PÁTZCUARO

One hour from Morelia is the colonial gem of Pátzcuaro. It is picture-postcard perfect, located in the highlands on a lake shore and overlooking a flotilla of small islands.

Pátzcuaro was the capital of the Purépecha people (called Tarascans by the Spanish), and the town is still home to many of the colourful Indian descendants, many of whom are skilled artisans and craftsmen. Thanks to Spanish Bishop Vasco de Quiroga, who encouraged education and rekindled the traditional crafts among the locals, the whole region is a good place to buy handicrafts. Visit the **Museo Regional de Pátzcuaro** or the **Museo de Artes Populares** for the background, and don't miss the **Casa de los Once Patios** (House of Eleven Patios), now a maze of handicraft shops offering a formidable diversity of quality items.

Tree-filled **Plaza Vasco de Quiroga**, the heart of town, is an impressive colonial square, while **Plaza Gertrudis Bocanegra** is just to the north. Don't miss the dark but bustling **market** on this square, with its cornucopia of regional handicrafts.

Janitzio ★

When in Pátzcuaro take a boat ride out on the lake itself: though the islands are rather dirty and very touristy, the trip is fun. The nearest island, Janitzio, is 20 minutes from Pátzcuaro. Look out for locals in small canoes fishing for *pescados blancos* with unusual butterfly-shaded nets. Restaurants around the lake serve this delicacy which, with increasing overfishing, is in danger of becoming a thing of the past.

TEQUILA TALES

Made from the grey **agave cactus**, tequila has its rituals. The first is that it is **never downed** in one, as mediocre movies would have us believe. It is a refined liquor and is usually drunk as an **aperitif**, either with a chunk of **lemon** and **salt** on the side, or as a **margarita** blended with triple sec, lime juice and salt. Aged tequila has much the same cachet as a fine brandy and can also be drunk after a meal. Tequila now finds its way into inventive modern **cuisine** in such dishes as flambéed prawns, ice sorbets and sauces. If you fancy visiting the best-known tequila distillery in Mexico, take a trip out to **El Cuervo**, in the town of **Tequila**, located just 56km (35 miles) northwest of Guadalajara.

Below: *Plaza de la Liberación, behind the cathedral, provides a welcome space for relaxation in the heart of Guadalajara.*

GUADALAJARA

Mexico's second-largest city and important tourist destination, Guadalajara has also attracted large numbers of foreign residents to its traditional colonial heart and its year-round temperate climate. It is smaller (though still boasts 5 million inhabitants) and less polluted than the capital, and many visitors find it much easier to get around and altogether more relaxing. It is as Mexican as cities come, and is renowned for its Mariachi music (immortalized in the song 'Guadalajara'), its tequila, the flamboyant *charro* costumes that go with the *charreada*, or Mexican rodeo, the wide-brimmed **sombrero** and, of course, the Mexican Hat Dance.

Laid out in an orderly fashion with plentiful parks, fountains, large shady boulevards and impressive historic buildings, Guadalajara merits spending a number of days to visit its major sites and to soak up the Tapotican atmosphere.

The **Catedral**, an imposing, architecturally varied structure with two solid spires, lies at the centre of old Guadalajara. Its cavernous pale interior is lavishly finished, reflecting the wealth of the city. Surrounding it are four large squares: **Plaza de la Rotunda** with its rotunda monument and statues of Jalisco's most famous sons; **Plaza de la Liberación** (which becomes the huge, pedestrian-only Plaza Tapatía to the east); **Plaza de las Armas** (the traditional *zócalo*, complete with delightful twice-weekly evening concerts and backed by the **Palacio del Gobierno**, with its extraordinary murals by Orozco); and **Plaza de los Laureles**, a formal square with many laurel trees and some cafés.

The most important sights include the **Teatro Degollado** – neo-Classical home to the Guadalajara Philharmonic Orchestra and the Ballet Folklórico; the neo-Classical **Instituto Cultural de Cabañas** with its 23 patios, once an orphanage, now a tourist attraction (admire the powerful

Orozco murals in the main chapel and visit the temporary art exhibitions); the **Museo Regional de Guadalajara** (noted for its paintings and archaeological exhibits); **Iglesia Santa Monica** and **Iglesia de San Francisco**; and the **Templo de Santa María de Gracia**, which was once the city's cathedral.

Late in the evenings music-lovers congregate in the **Plaza de los Mariachis** to listen to strolling Mariachi bands, who serenade an appreciative audience in return for a few dollars.

The fun-loving Tapatícos ensure that evenings in Guadalajara remain vibrant. Cinema, theatre and folk ballet are all readily available, and music is heard all around town in bars and cafés.

Above: *Though the music of Mariachi players can be heard all over Mexico, it originated in Guadalajara.*

Excursions

Once independent of Guadalajara, **Tlaquepaque** and **Tonalá** (weekly markets on Thursdays and Sundays) are now suburbs worth visiting for their vast range of arts and crafts. They are a shopper's delight.

Lake Chapala, Mexico's biggest lake, is sitauted just some 40km (25 miles) south of Guadalajara. Its enviable climate and beautiful setting have attracted hundreds of North American retirees.

MARIACHI MANIA

Throughout Mexico, you will come across Mariachis. A group of **wandering musicians** playing guitars and trumpets, dressed in traditional black with broad-brimmed sombreros, the Mariachis have a debated origin. Were they a feature before the **Spanish** arrived, did they take their name from the corruption of the name for the bands that played at marriages during the brief **French** reign, or did their name come from the stage on which the *jabarabe* was danced? It matters little. The Mariachi band is an integral part of Mexico and there is nowhere better to enjoy their traditional Mexican ballads than in **Guadalajara's Plaza de los Mariachis**.

Central Guadalajara

QUERÉTARO

Located approximately two hours north of Mexico City in the central highlands is the city of Querétaro, capital of the state of the same name. The charming old city centre, founded in 1559 on the site of a lucrative silver mine, is a veritable architectural treasure and UNESCO has designated it a **World Heritage Site**. Authentic colonial mansions (a number of which have been converted into hotels), pedestrian-only streets and shady squares transport today's visitor right into the pages of the city's rich history. Very much 20th-century, however, is the highly respected annual **Cervantes Festival**. This wonderful fortnight-long event is held each October and transforms the city into a stage for world-class arts and music.

Top sights in Querétaro include the **Iglesia de San Francisco** on the **Plaza Principal** or **Jardín Obregón**, which houses the **Museo Regional de Querétaro** with its marvellous historic documents and paintings. Other museums in the city include the **Museo de la Ciudad** and the **Museo de Arte de Querétaro**. Situated just two blocks east of the main square, the **Palacio del Gobierno del Estado**, home of Doña Josefa Ortiz, was the place where the Independence movement was born. Nearby, don't miss the beautiful Baroque façade of the **Casa del Escala**. Outside town, the 74-arch **aqueduct** is an impressive site (imaginatively lit by night), while the **Cerro de las Campanas**, now a park, marks the spot where Maximilian was executed.

If in any way possible, try to plan a visit to coincide with Querétaro's annual **Feria**, one of Mexico's biggest exhibitions, during early December.

CHURRIGUERESQUE DECORATION

The Churrigueresque style (named for the Spanish Catalan architect, **José de Churriguera**) is a peculiar Mexican characteristic and one which you find in many of the churches built during colonial days. Churriguera developed this elaborate, **three-dimensional** style for decorating his religious commissions. The best examples of his work include: **Iglesia de San Francisco Javier** in Tepotzotlán; the **Santuario de la Virgen de Ocotlán** in Tlaxcala; the **cathedral** in Zacatecas and the façade of the **Sagrario**, in Mexico City.

SAN MIGUEL DE ALLENDE

Approximately an hour from Querétaro, San Miguel de Allende enjoys a mild, sunny climate and has attracted scores of foreign artists, musicians and craftsmen to live and work in its picturesque cobbled streets and colourful colonial buildings. Such is its overall attraction that UNESCO designated the entire town of San Miguel de Allende a **World Heritage Site** in 1926.

There is not one great monument here, but dozens of smaller sights, and the attraction lies in discovering these by wandering through the streets or having your visit coincide with one of the many exuberant **local fiestas**. Here you can learn to speak Spanish, take up an art or dance course, or immerse yourself in Mexican culture. Contact the **Instituto de Allende** and the **Bellas Artes Cultural Center** for details.

The **Plaza Principal** (also known as the **Jardín** or Plaza Allende after local hero and freedom fighter, Ignacio Allende) is the pivot point for exploration; on the southern side of the Plaza you will find **La Parroquia** (arguably even more beautiful by night), the pink parish church – an ornate quasi-Gothic structure with the most extraordinary soaring towers (conceived by a self-taught Indian architect who also designed the **Iglesia de la Concepción**) – and, next to it, **Iglesia San Rafael**. For an overall view of the town, visit the **mirador** near the Parque Benito Juárez. The local *señoras* at the **lavandería** (the public washtubs) at **El Chorro** are an interesting sight in the morning.

San Miguel is a wonderful place to be if you are looking for good quality **handi-crafts**. The **Mercado de Artesanías** has rather a good selection, but your best bet would be to search the art shops that are dotted around the main square.

DOLORES HIDALGO

Just 40km (25 miles) from San Miguel de Allende, Dolores Hidalgo is worth a visit if time permits. Not only is it the **birthplace** of the **modern Mexican nation**, thanks to the Independence movement initiated by Father Miguel Hidalgo, but it is also renowned for its **pottery** and home-made **ice cream**. These ice creams feature those fruity tastes that we know so well, but also come in whiskey, alfalfa, coconut, tequila and shrimp flavours!

Opposite: *Silver mining put Querétaro on the map.*
Below: *Crafts for sale in San Miguel de Allende.*

ZACATECAS

Zacatecas is a wealthy, elegant city of beautiful colonial buildings set in an arid yet appealing landscape. Although it rests in a valley between two peaks, its heart lies around the *zócalo*, **Plaza de Armas**. Here bands play rousing marches, sombrero-clad elders in cowboy boots gather, and early each day solitary peasants lead their donkeys laden with pottery jars of *aguamiel*, a sweet drink. This is where the pink Baroque **Catedral** (possibly the most beautiful in Mexico) is situated, a building which takes the Churrigueresque style to its dizziest heights. The adjacent **Palacio de Gobierno** holds a series of frescoes portraying the history of Zacatecas. The pink stone **Palacio de la Mala Noche**, nearby, was owned by a silver magnate. The **Iglesia de San Agustín** and the **Templo de Santo Domingo** are two fine churches, while the iron-columned **Mercado González Ortega**, previously the city's main market, has been renovated to offer a selection of upmarket shops and restaurants.

The city's best hotel, the architecturally stunning **Quinta Real**, has the unusual distinction of being integrated into what was previously a bull ring.

Museo Pedro Coronel, named after the renowned artist who left his home as well as a superb private collection of paintings to Zacatecas, is a must. So, too, is the **Museo Rafael Coronel** (housed in the ex-Convento de San Francisco), with its 3000 Mexican masks.

For 400 years, **Mina El Edén** was one of the country's most active mines. The mine is open to tourists, and a visit is an interesting experience.

For a breathtaking view of town and the surrounding countryside, take the *teleférico* to the top of **Cerro de la Bufa**, the rocky outcrop which overlooks Zacatecas.

Left: *Dusk falls over the multicoloured town of Guanajuato.*
Opposite: *This distinctive building, once a bullring, has now been converted into the luxury Quinta Real Hotel, Zacatecas,*
Below: *Like its Bolivian namesake, Potosí is known for its silver mining.*

GUANAJUATO

Coming northwest from Mexico City, it is a pretty four-hour drive here through semi-arid hills and mountains. Situated in a gorge, Guanajuato is constructed on various levels and ideal for the energetic walker. A more colourful town you could hardly imagine. Earth-coloured limestone walls, pastel buildings, old fountains and welcome wrought-iron benches, frivolously decorated churches, hidden courtyards, endless flights of steps – this city is a photographer's paradise and another UNESCO World Heritage Site. In addition, many of the through roads have been built underground, making a pedestrian's life more pleasant.

Focal point of this elongated town is the triangular **Jardín de la Unión**. The **Teatro Juárez** nearby is a marvel. An old granary turned art museum, the **Alhóndiga de Granaditas** played an important role in the War of Independence, when Hidalgo and his followers smoked out and then killed many of the thousands of Spanish soldiers barricaded within. Museums include the **Museo Diego Rivera** – the house in which this great artist was born and now a museum with furniture and works of art – and the extraordinary **Museo de Las Momias** (a collection of mummified bodies). Slightly out of the centre the **ex-Hacienda Barrera** (a hacienda museum with fine gardens), the impressive **Templo de San Cayetano** (the Valencia, on the site of the **Mina Valencia**), and the mine itself are all worth a visit.

SAN LUÍS POTOSÍ

A historical colonial town in the northern part of central Mexico, San Luís Potosí was an important **silver** town and its colonial heart still remains intact despite its expanding suburbs. It was called Potosí after the **Bolivian** silvermining town of the same name – the **conquistadors** hoped this town would prove as lucrative as the other. Ultimately it was not and it rebuilt its wealth on **cattle** and, later, **manufacturing**.

Central Highlands at a Glance

BEST TIMES TO VISIT

Although **Nov** to **Apr** are the driest months of the year, almost any time of the year is pleasant. Night temperatures are cool but the days are agreeably warm.

GETTING THERE

Guadalajara, Zacatecas, San Luís Potosí, Querétaro and Morelia all have airports. Long-distance buses in all classes operate from the capital and between many of the cities.

GETTING AROUND

Walking is the most effective way of getting around as the historic centres are compact. In Guadalajara it is also easy to use the bus, metro or taxi.

WHERE TO STAY

LUXURY

Hotel Villa Montana, Patzimba 201, Morelia, tel: (43) 14-0231, fax: 15-1423. Hacienda-style garden hotel overlooking the city.
Hotel Fiesta Americana, Aurelio Aceves 225, Guadalajara, tel: (3) 625-3434, fax: 830-3725. Strikingly modern hotel with full amenities.
Hotel Quinta Real, Av Mexico 2727, Guadalajara, tel: (3) 134-2424, fax: 134-2404. Suites hotel with colonial ambience.
Hotel Camino Real, Av Vallarta 5005, Guadalajara, tel: (3) 121-8000, fax: 121-8070. Luxury accommodation in residential area.

Hotel Mesón de Santa Rosa, Pasteur Sur 17, Querétaro, tel: (42) 24-2623, fax: 12-5522. Central, recently converted.
Hotel Casa de Sierra Nevada, Hospicio 35, San Miguel de Allende, tel: (415) 27040, fax: 21436. Colonial, central, award-winning restaurants.
Hotel Quinta Real, Zacatecas, tel: (492) 29104, fax: 28440. An architectural gem, built into a bullring.
Hotel Continental Plaza, Av Hidalgo 703, Zacatecas, tel: (492) 26183, fax: 26245. Colonial hotel in local pink stone, good restaurant.

MID-RANGE

Hotel Virrey de Mendoza, Avenida Madero Poniente 310, Morelia, tel: (43) 12-4940. Centrally located, colonial.
Hotel Mansión Iturbe, Portal Morelos 59, Pátzcuaro, tel: (434) 20368, fax: 13-4593. Delightful B&B inn on central square.
Plaza Génova Best Western, Av Juárez 12, Guadalajara, tel: (3) 613-7500, fax: 614-8253. Centrally located.
Holiday Inn, Av Lopez Mateos Sur 2500, Guadalajara, tel: (3) 634-1034, fax: 631-9395. Modern hotel.
Hotel Mirabel, Constituyentes Orente 2, Querétaro, tel: (42) 14-3535, fax: 14-3585. Centrally located, friendly.
Hotel Pensión Casa Carmen, Correo 31, San Miguel de Allende, tel and fax: (415) 20844. Converted colonial building, repeat clientele.

Posada Santa Fé, Unión 12, Guanajuato, tel: (473) 20084, fax: 24653. Longest standing central city hotel, colonial comfort, good Mexican restaurant.

BUDGET

Hotel Fénix, Madero Poniente 537, Morelia, tel: (43) 12-0512. Basic, clean, central location.
Posada San Rafael, Plaza Vasco de Quiroga, Pátzcuaro, tel: (434) 20770. Bright, comfortable and very central.
Hotel Francés, Maestranza 355, Guadalajara, tel: (3) 613-1190, fax: 658-2831. Historic colonial hotel in centre.
Hotel Hidalgo, Madero 11 Poniente, Querétaro, tel: (42) 12-0081. Very central, basic.
Hotel Quinta Loreto, Calle Loreto 15, San Miguel de Allende, tel: (415) 20042, fax: 23616. Good restaurant.
Hotel Posada de los Condes, Juárez 107, Zacatecas, tel: (492) 21093. Colonial building, good location with pleasant rooms.
Hostería del Frayle, Sopeña 3, Guanajuato, tel: (473) 21179. Good rooms, friendly, central.

WHERE TO EAT

LUXURY

Restaurant Bugambilia, Hidalgo 42, San Miguel de Allende, tel: (415) 20127. Mexican cuisine, live music.

MID-RANGE

Fonda las Mercedes, Calle León Guzmán 47, Morelia, tel: (434) 24240. Mexican and international cuisine.

Central Highlands at a Glance

El Patio, Plaza Vasco de Quiroga 19, Pátzcuaro, tel: (434) 20-4848. International and Mexican cuisine.
La Fonda de San Miguel, Donato Guerra 25, Guadalajara, tel: (3) 613-0809. Good ambience, Mexican cuisine.
La Feria, Corona 291 (Esq. Héroes), Guadalajara, tel: (3) 613-1812. Mexican food.
Casco Viejo, Av México 2742, Guadalajara, tel: (3) 616-5787. Good Mexican cuisine.
Restaurant Mama Mia, Calle de Umarán 8, San Miguel de Allende, tel: (415) 22063. Italian and Mexican cuisine, good music, very popular.
La Cantera Musical, Tacuba 2 (under the market), tel: 922 8828. Mexican cuisine, good wine cellar.
Restaurant Parrilla Bar, local 6, El Mercado, Zacatecas, tel: (492) 21433. Young, trendy, good food and antojitos.
El Santuario, Jardín de la Unión 4, Guanajuato. Trendy restaurant, open late. Mexican and international cuisine.
Hotel San Diego, Jardín de la Unión, tel: (473) 21300, Guanajuato. Smart restaurant, good Mexican food.

BUDGET
Restaurant Los Itacates, Chapultepec 110, Guadalajara, tel: (3) 825-1106. Good quality and value. Mexican cuisine.
Mesón de Chucho El Roto, Plaza de la Independencia, Querétaro. Serves good Mexican cuisine.

Pastelería Francesa, Mesones, San Miguel de Allende. Excellent French-style pastries are available here.
La Galería and **La Guitarra**, Guanajuato. Both good bars with antojitos and music. Open till late.

SHOPPING

In **Morelia** is Casa de las Artisanías. Casa de los Once Patios in **Pátzcuaro** sells handicrafts. Good boots and shoes can be found around the Plaza Galería del Calzada in **Guadalajara**. **San Miguel de Allende** is good for clothing, unusual jewellery, and arts and crafts. Try Mercado de Artisanías for inexpensive items. **Zacatecas** is known for leather and silver. Plaza Genaro Codina is the best place to shop here. You will find silverware in **Guanajuato**.

TOURS AND EXCURSIONS

Morelia: Trips to Monarch Butterfly Sanctuary, El Rosario.
Guadalajara: Panoramex, tel: (3) 810-5109, for excursions including local sights, Chapala, Ajijic and Tequila to see liquor production. Also local trips to Tonalá and Tlaquepaque.
San Miguel de Allende: Trips to hot springs: Taboada, Pozos and Parador del Cortijo.

USEFUL CONTACTS

Oficina de Turismo:
Morelia: Calle Nigromante 79, tel: (43) 12-8081.
Pátzcuaro: Plaza Vasco de Quiroga, tel: (434) 21214.
Guadalajara: Calle Morelos 102, tel: (3) 616-3332.
Querétaro: Pasteur Norte 4, tel: (42) 12-1412.
San Miguel de Allende: Plaza Principal, tel: (415) 21747.
Zacatecas: Av Hidalgo and Callejón de Santero, tel: (492) 44047.
Guanajuato: Plaza de la Paz 14, tel: (473) 21982.

Others:
Aeroméxico: Corona 196, Guadalajara, tel: (3) 688-5098.
Mexicana: Otero 2353, Guadalajara, tel: (3) 112-0011.
Language courses at San Miguel de Allende: Bellas Artes Cultural Center, tel: (415) 20289, Dr. Hernández Macías no. 75; Instituto de Allende, Ancha de San Antonio no. 20, tel: (415) 20190, fax: 24538.
Language courses at Guanajuato: University of Guanajuato, Lascuraín de Rentana 7, tel: (473) 20006.

GUADALAJARA	J	F	M	A	M	J	J	A	S	O	N	D
AVERAGE TEMP. °F	75	77	81	86	91	86	81	80	79	78	77	75
AVERAGE TEMP. °C	24	25	27	30	33	30	27	26	26	26	25	24
RAINFALL in	1	0.5	0.1	-	-	-	1	2	2.5	1	2	1
RAINFALL mm	12	12	4	-	-	-	13	44	51	12	39	13

6
The Pacific Coast

No other country in the northern hemisphere has as long and varied a coastline as Mexico. From the mouth of the Colorado River to the border with Guatemala, over 3500km (2175 miles) of shore – much of it subtropical – has for decades enticed visitors south of the border to smart resorts. And, despite the developments elsewhere in Mexico, the Pacific coast not only remains a favourite (especially with North Americans), but it continues to develop resorts along previously untouched shores. This part of Mexico was lashed by the severe storms associated with Hurricane Paulina in 1997 but it has bounced back with even more vigor and enthusiasm. Indeed, damaged cities and hotels were obliged to re-evaluate their strengths and weaknesses and have since capitalized on what might have been a disaster, rebuilding and renovating certain areas.

The older, established resorts – **Puerto Vallarta**, **Acapulco** and fishing port-cum-resort **Mazatlán** – have all grown old graciously and stretched out on either side to form newer, satellite resorts. Other world-class newcomers include the resort of **Ixtapa** and the older fishing village of **Zihuatanejo**.

This is an ideal spot for sun-lovers and pleasure-seekers. Along the Pacific coast are endless sandy beaches where swimming is safe, and scuba diving, snorkelling and game fishing are popular pastimes. Other sporting options include hiking, horseback riding, golf and tennis. For a taste of sophisticated nightlife, the older resorts are well worth a visit.

DON'T MISS

*** Acapulco: glittering star of the coast, with its night and day attractions.
*** La Quebrada: divers plunge from great heights into the ocean.
*** Puerto Vallarta: a fun resort with plenty to do.
** Zihuatanejo: a fishing town turned smart resort.
** Snorkel or scuba: diving trips to offshore islands are a great day away.
** Sublime seafood: in Mazatlán or Puerto Vallarta.

Opposite: *Hotel Quinta Real on the beautiful long beach, Playa Revolcadero, near Acapulco.*

Above: *One of Puerto Vallarta's favourite swimming beaches, Playa de los Muertos attracts crowds of tourists and locals alike to its pleasant shores.*

MAZATLÁN

One of the first resorts to be developed on the Pacific coast, Mazatlán has matured gracefully. It is the coast's most important fishing port (it is also Mexico's prawn capital) and revered for its game fishing. Although many tourists come here by road and plane, many others visit by cruise ship.

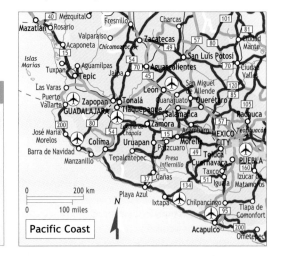

CLIMATE

November to **April** are the driest months along the Pacific coast, but temperatures are high year-round, averaging 32°C (90°F) during the day and 24°C (75°F) at night. The peak season is during the **winter**, when the top resorts are packed with tourists seeking sun, sand and entertainment.

The settlement was founded in 1531, though it was some 300 years before a permanent colony was established. The older part of town is in the south while the newest resorts spread out along the northern shores in front of the three small offshore islands, and the *malecón* (seafront promenade) runs over 16km (10 miles) between the two areas. Buses are frequent and easy to negotiate.

The centre of the old town is the **Plaza Principal** with its **Catedral**. This is the focal point for the annual **Carnival** celebration, one of Mexico's most colourful. Nearby are the **Palacio Municipal** and the pink **Teatro Angela Peralta**. For a different angle on Mazatlán, a visit to **El Faro**, the world's second-tallest lighthouse, located south of *Mazatlán Viejo*, is impressive.

The best beaches are always debatable. Most prefer those in the **Zona Dorada**, the touristy central belt. These beaches – **Playa Camarón**, **Playa Gaviota** and **Playa Sábalo** – are sheltered by the offshore isles. Better still are the beaches on these three islands; boats make the crossing three times daily. North of the **Marina del Sábalo**, the beach is even less crowded and worth the bus trip.

Night-time Mazatlán also has much to offer, with its restaurants, cafés and discotheques.

Puerto Vallarta

A mere couple of decades ago, sophisticated, expensive Puerto Vallarta was just a quaint little fishing village on the magnificent **Bahía de las Banderas**. Movies, however, changed all that. In the wake of *The Night of the Iguana*, and the arrival of luminaries such as Richard Burton and Liz Taylor, condominiums, time-share, luxury hotels and villas have given Puerto Vallarta a new attitude to life. Some of the old buildings in the original town have been altered to become fashionable restaurants, art galleries and souvenir shops, while the sandy central beaches along the 150km (93-mile) shore of Bahía de las Banderas have become favourites for daily cruise excursions.

Below: *Tourists can visit the location where 'The Night of the Iguana' was filmed in Mismaloya, Puerto Vallarta.*

Below right: *Puerto
Vallarta has now expanded
into Marina Vallarta and
Nueva Vallarta.*

On either side of the Río Cuale, old Puerto Vallarta
is the commercial centre of this pretty town. A lovely
malécon, or promenade, provides a focal point each
evening for strollers and itinerant vendors. There are
galleries, cafés, shops and a small **Museo Arqueológico**.
The shady **Plaza de Armas** is the main square or *zócalo*.
Here the **Palacio Municipal** houses the tourist office,
while a block to the east is the **Iglesia de Nuestra Señora
de Guadalupe** with its unusual tower. The annual
fiesta of the **Virgin of Guadalupe** (12 December) is particularly riotous here, with more than ten days of
celebrations. Other notable dates include the **Semana
Santa** celebrations, the annual fishing tournament in
November, and the biennial **Regatta** between the
Marina del Rey (San Diego) and Puerto Vallarta.

Mariachi, indeed all music, is big in Puerto Vallarta,
and there are a number of local restaurants where live
Mariachi music accompanies dinner. Catering to the
diner who wants a touch of Mexican culture with a
buffet, the long-standing **La Iguana** offers nightly shows,
as do many of the luxury hotels.

Day cruises, complete with meals, drinks and music,
set out each day to cross the bay, sail into the sunset
and cruise under the stars; there are also trips for divers
and snorkellers to the protected ecological zone of **Los
Arcos**, the large boulders which lie offshore from **Playa
Mismaloya**. With their reefs and walls, the **Islas
Marietas**, too, are a good place for scuba divers and
snorkellers to discover dolphins, whales and rays.

Other sporting options include **hiking** or **horseback riding** along the jungle paths in the hills behind Puerto Vallarta, as well as **golf** and **tennis** – the former in the smart Marina Vallarta Golf Club and the latter at the same address or at John Newcombe Tennis Club. Most of the luxury hotels also have tennis courts.

Puerto Vallarta is expanding northwards. **Marina Vallarta** is its thriving port and yacht harbour with a sprinkling of luxurious hotels, while **Nueva Vallarta** capitalizes on its beautiful beaches, and a backdrop of impressive mountains clothed in semitropical vegetation, to create another new destination.

Above: *Cruising Puerto Vallarta's magnificent bay at sunset is a fine way to round off the day.*

MANZANILLO

Mexicans (and well-heeled foreign holiday-makers) have a penchant for Manzanillo which was, and still is, a busy port. It developed around two sandy bays, **Bahía de Santiago** and the main **Bahía de Manzanillo**, separated by the **Santiago Peninsula**. Downtown Manzanillo holds little of interest: tourists come here for the beach and because John Derek's film *10* starring his wife, Bo Derek, was filmed at the exquisite **Las Hadas** resort here. There are a dozen beaches of both white and black sand where the swimming is safe and the snorkelling and diving are good. Game-fishing enthusiasts should time a visit to coincide with the international **sailfish tournament** held annually in November. Tuna, yellowtail and other game fish are also prolific in the winter months.

Costa Careyes ★

Between Manzanillo and Puerto Vallarta, along hundreds of kilometres of pristine coast, a few exclusive hideaways are making a name for themselves. The most popular are in the **Costa Careyes** area, where world-class architects have melded tropical Mexico with Mediterranean chic to form some superb private and hotel properties.

MEXICAN MEALS

Mexicans eat at least three times a day. They start with a *desayuno* (breakfast) of sweet buns and coffee or chocolate when they rise. Mid-morning, they might have a substantial meal of eggs, beans and tortillas. The *comida* (main meal) is eaten in the afternoon between 13:00 and 17:00. A small *merienda* (snack) is often eaten in the evening and, on special occasions, *cena* (dinner) follows, which could go on to midnight, or longer.

Above: *New holiday homes and hotels are sprouting along the Mexican coast north of Acapulco and south of Ixtapa.*
Opposite: *Turtles often make the soft sandy shore their nesting place. These reptiles are, today, protected.*

Colima ★

An excursion to Colima – 45km (28 miles) inland from Manzanillo – is an interesting contrast to beach life. This colonial city has few original buildings as earthquakes and eruptions from the Volcán de Fuego de Colima destroyed most. Indeed, the volcano often threatens the city and surrounding areas. But its **Museo de Historia de Colima** on the south side of the **Plaza Principal** merits a visit for the ceramics – delightful figurines (dogs and people) unearthed in the state of Colima. These sturdy canines were bred as a food source. The **Palacio de Gobierno** and (relatively modern) **Catedral** are also nearby.

Playa Azul ★

Just inside the state of Michoacán, near Lázaro Cárdenas, Playa Azul is a popular holiday resort for Mexicans. The beach is often empty during the week but come the weekend the town pads out. Like other areas on this Pacific coast, the surf can be rough and sea swimming is not always advisable. However, for a taste of Mexican Mexico, Playa Azul is fun.

SWEET INDULGENCES

Colima is noted for its sweet candy, **cocada**. Made from a delicious mixture of local coconut, sugar and milk, it can be found in shops throughout the city.

IXTAPA AND ZIHUATANEJO

A stretch of palm-fringed shore (Ixtapa) and a traditional fishing village (Zihuatanejo) just 8km (5 miles) apart have been developed into one of Mexico's most popular resorts. Ixtapa is flamboyant, modern and architecturally coordinated. Zihuatanejo is still quaint, holding onto its traditions, but has been gentrified with small exclusive boutiques and smart restaurants along its **Paseo de Pescador**. Both have their followers.

The setting for this resort is perfect. An assortment of luxury hotels lies alongside the clean (though not always calm) waters of the Bahía de Palmar, while in Bahía de Zihuatanejo some exquisite little hotels are hidden behind the fishing boats.

The beach is the prime reason to come here. In Zihuatanejo, **Playa Las Gatas** (accessible by boat) is a popular spot, the **Playa Principal** is the busy central beach, while **Playa Madera** and **Playa La Ropa** are good swimming beaches. Ixtapa's long beach, the **Bahía de Palmar**, is open to all, but visitors also opt to visit the **Isla Ixtapa** – an offshore wildlife preserve where swimming, scuba diving and snorkelling can be great. Game fishing is also popular: marlin, wahoo, dorado and Spanish mackerel all lure aficionados. Make enquiries at the **Marina**.

Golf, too, is popular: there are two 18-hole courses open to nonmembers. As an antidote to all these sports, the resorts have good shopping. The **Mercado de Artesanías Turístico** is a convenient place to see a range of goods.

As you would expect, restaurants in this twin resort are excellent, with a great array of fish and seafood. Leave time to indulge. Many of the larger hotels offer **Fiestas Mexicanas** in the evening for a potpourri of Mexican music and dance.

TURTLES

Turtles are a **protected species**. Mexico has seven of the world's eight species and serious efforts are being made in various parts of the country to ensure that their eggs and nests are not destroyed by unscrupulous egg collectors. The most common turtles are the **olive ridley**, **green turtle** and **loggerhead**. Female turtles are thought to return to the same beach where they themselves were hatched.

Turtles are found along many of Mexico's sandy beaches. Females lumber ashore during the **breeding season**, heaving themselves up to beyond the high tide mark, dig a hole with their flippers and lay from 50 to 200 golfball-sized **eggs**. In the process they shed tears – not because of the effort or emotional reasons, but to keep the sand from their eyes. Then they pad back to the sea. Some 6–10 weeks later the **hatchlings** scrabble their way to the surface and make a mad dash to the sea, where a whole host of **predators** await. It is estimated that only 1 per cent of hatchlings make it to adulthood.

LA QUEBRADA

Five times daily, **divers** thrill visitors with their graceful dives from the 40m (131ft) **cliffs** into the churning sea below. This **tradition** dates back to 1934 and is particularly impressive at sunset and later in the evening, when the divers hold torches. The **Restaurant La Perla** (Plaza Las Glorias Hotel) conveniently combines dining with diving.

Opposite: *Playa Hornitos, one of the most popular beaches in Acapulco.*
Below: *Five times daily Quebrada divers leap into a turbulent sea.*

ACAPULCO

In the mid-17th century, Acapulco was a port of call for ships laden with ivory, silks and porcelain on their route between the Philippines and Spain. Today's vessels carry tourists who cruise from one Pacific port to another. Situated between sea and sierra, Acapulco has a magnificent position. It boasts 15 beaches around its deep bay and two headlands with offshore isles. Between the headlands a city of over a million people thrives. Long the glittering star of the Pacific coast, Acapulco is making a comeback after the hurricane damage in late 1997.

In the daytime, it is the beaches that lure visitors. **Playa Condesa** and **Playa Hornitos** are two of the best beaches, while families prefer the protected **Playa Caleta** and **Playa Caletilla** and the beaches on the offshore isle, **Isla la Roqueta**. Behind the city beaches are lagoons – ideal for **waterskiing**. Other sporting activities include **scuba diving** (it is a great place to learn the basics), snorkelling, **deep-sea fishing** and windsurfing. Shotover Jet (*see page 93*) offer high-speed trips down the **Río Papagayo** providing thrills for those with nerves of steel.

Tennis and golf enthusiasts are well catered for (there are four 18-hole championship golf courses and one nine-hole links), while spectator sports include Sunday **bullfighting** during the Fiesta Brava season, from November to April. Acapulco turns party city when it hosts its **Acapulco Festival** in the second week of May, inviting international and local musicians to participate.

After exploring the pirate-filled museum in **Fuerte de San Diego** and passing the glorious **Rivera** ceramic mural outside **Dolores Olmedo's** house, there is not very much more old culture in Acapulco but certainly plenty of new.

You could while away hours shopping in the malls, boutiques or markets (the **Mercado de Artesanías** is tops for handicrafts), or marvel at the tropical fish and shark feeding in the aquarium, **Mágico Mundo Marino**. Acapulco has several amusements for children (of all ages) including the **CICI** water park.

A trip to see the famous **Quebrada** divers flinging themselves from the cliffs into the ocean is a must. They perform five times daily.

Come nightfall, Acapulco positively scintillates: over 150 restaurants offer menus from around the world as well as local seafood specialities, there are scores of lively bars and cafés, and the futuristic discos pack in stars and holiday-makers alike.

On the road between the airport and Acapulco (but developing under a separate name) is **Acapulco Diamante**, situated on the sheltered bay of **Puerto Marquéz** and the endless **Revolcadero Beach**. The beaches here are gorgeous, and suitably beautiful homes and hotels are now appearing amid the tropical landscape.

Excursions from Acapulco should include a visit to **Pie de la Cuesta** and the **Laguna de Coyuca**, with its wealth of waterbirds. Alternatively, the **Tres Palos** freshwater lagoons are also good for birdlife and swimming.

PIRATES AND THE PAST

When **Cortés** arrived in **Acapulco** in 1530, he recognized its potential and established a **ship-building centre**. This once sleepy village soon became a staging point on the lucrative **trade route** between the Philippines and Spain. Laden with cargoes of silk, silver, ivory and porcelain, the ships were preyed upon by such pirates as **Sir Francis Drake**. To ward off these bounty hunters, the Spanish built the **Fort of San Diego**. But in 1818 it was besieged by Mexican troops and the Spanish left, taking their profitable trade with them. It was not until **American luminaries** and **movie stars** began to spend time in the town that Acapulco regained its importance.

The Pacific Coast at a Glance

BEST TIMES TO VISIT

Nov to **Apr** is best, but resorts like Acapulco, Puerto Vallarta and Ixtapa thrive year round.

GETTING THERE

All main cities are accessible by **air** from the capital and the US. **Buses** from Mexico City serve all the resorts mentioned and ply the Pacific coast between Mazatlán and Salina Cruz.

GETTING AROUND

Visitors can **hire cars** and **motorbikes** in the major towns. **Buses** or **peseros** are reliable in all the towns. **Walking** is best.

WHERE TO STAY

There are dozens of deluxe hotels, many mid-range hotels and rather fewer budget ones. We give just the briefest of recommendations here.

LUXURY

Fiesta Inn, Av Camarón Sábalo 1927, Mazatlán, tel: (69) 89-0103, fax: 89-0130. Beachside hotel, on lovely northern shores of town.
Sheraton Buganvilias, Bvd F. Medina Ascencio 999, Puerto Vallarta, tel: (322) 60404, fax: 20500. Slightly out of town, but walkable.
Fiesta Americana, Blvd Francisco Medina Ascencio, Puerto Vallarta, tel: (322) 42010, fax: 42108. Near town, on beach.
The Careyes, Costa Careyes (between Puerto Vallarta and Manzanillo), tel: (335) 10000, fax: 10100. Hideaway resort of

private homes, villas and hotel.
Camino Real Las Hadas, Rincón de las Hadas, Manzanillo, tel: (333) 42000, fax: 41370. Fabulous Moorish villa hotel.
La Casa Que Canta, Playa la Ropa, Zihuatanejo, tel: (755) 57030, fax: 47900. Exclusive, constructed in local materials.
Westin Brisas Resort Ixtapa, Playa Vista Hermosa, Ixtapa, tel: (755) 32121, fax: 30751. Good restaurants, tranquil rooms.
Camino Real Acapulco Diamante, Baja Catita, Acapulco, tel: (74) 66-1010, fax: 66-1111. New, colonial-style hotel, own private cove, a few kilometres from centre. Good restaurants.
Fiesta Americana Condesa, Costera M. Alemán 1220, Acapulco, tel: (74) 84-2828, fax: 84-2936. Very popular, on one of the best beaches.
Elcano, Av Costera M. Alemán 75, Acapulco, tel: (74) 84-1950, fax: 84-2230. Lovely tropical gardens, excellent restaurants.

MID-RANGE

Aguamarina Hotel, Av del Mar 110, Mazatlán, tel: (69) 81-7080, fax: 82-4624. Renovated, very popular; has own pool and restaurant.
Molino de Agua, Vallarta 130, Puerto Vallarta, tel: (322) 21907, fax: 26056. Bungalow hotel, lovely gardens, central.
Hotel Playa Azul, Carranza, Playa Azul, Manzanillo, tel and fax: (333) 32712. Best town hotel with popular restaurant.
Hotel Paraíso Real, Playa la Ropa, Zihuatanejo, tel and fax:

(755) 43873. Small hotel, near beach. Scuba diving available.
Boca Chica Hotel, Playa Caletilla 7, Acapulco, tel: (740) 83-6741, fax: 83-9513. Small hotel on own cove, good views, friendly staff and peaceful.
Park Motel Acapulco, Av Costera M. Alemán 127, Acapulco, tel: (74) 85-5437, fax: 85-5489. Clean, comfortable.

BUDGET

La Siesta, Olas Altas 11, Mazatlán, tel: (69) 13-4655. Just across road from beach.
Hotel Eloísa, Lázaro Cárdenas 179, Puerto Vallarta, tel: (322) 26465, fax: 20268. Near beach, very well established.
Hotel Colonial, Bocanegra 100, Manzanillo, tel: (333) 21080. Traditional (stained-glass windows, high ceilings) and popular. Good restaurant.
Hotel Avila, Juan Alvarez 8, Zihuatanejo, tel: (755) 42010. Friendly, overlooking beach.
Hotel Misión, Felipe Valle 12, Acapulco, tel: (74) 82-3643. Charming hotel near *zócalo*.

WHERE TO EAT

LUXURY

Hotel Playa Mazatlán's *Fiesta Mexicana* (see page 89). Thrice-weekly folkloric dance show with dinner buffet.
Trio, Guerrero 264, Puerto Vallarta, tel: (322) 22196. Innovative Mediterranean cuisine.
Archie's Wok, Francisca Rodríguez 130, Puerto Vallarta, tel: (322) 20411. Well-known, Thai and Pacific Rim cuisine.

Villa de la Selva, Paseo de la Roca, Ixtapa, tel: (755) 30362. Fine food, international menu.
Kau-Kan, Playa Madera, Zihuatanejo, tel: (755) 48446. Popular, innovative cuisine.
El Olvido, Plaza Marbella, Costera M Alemán, Acapulco, tel: (74) 81-0214. Tropical beach location, inventive cuisine.
Spicey, Carretera Escénica, Acapulco, tel: (74) 46-6003. Trendy people-watching place. Pacific rim, European cuisine.
Zapata, Villa y Compañía, Hyatt Regency Acapulco, Av Costera M. Alemán, Acapulco, tel: (74) 69-1234. Good décor. Excellent Mexican cuisine.

MID-RANGE
El Shrimp Bucket, Olas Altas 11, Mazatlán. Mexican and international, lots of seafood.
Planet Hollywood and **Hard Rock Café**, Puerto Vallarta, are branches of the popular chains. Mexican, international dishes.
Carlos' n' Charlie's, Costera Madrid, Manzanillo, tel: (333) 31150. Mexican, international.
La Cabaña de Caleta, Playa Caleta, Acapulco, tel: (74) 82-5007. Excellent seafood, overlooking the beach.
100% Natural, Acapulco. Five healthy eating cafés around town. Inexpensive to moderate.

BUDGET
Café de Olla, Badillo 168, Puerto Vallarta. Grills, Mexican cuisine.
Casa Elvira, Paseo del Pescador, Zihuatanejo, tel: (755)

42061. Long-time favourite. Seafood and Mexican cuisine.

SHOPPING

Centro Commercial El Mercado in **Mazatlán** sells leather, silver, vanilla, pottery. Try Mercado Municipal in **Puerto Vallarta** for handicrafts. Agustín Rodríguez also has attractive shops. In **Ixtapa-Zihuatanejo** are the Mercado Túristico, 5 de Mayo or Mercado de las Artesanías. Plata de Taxco has a selection of Taxco silver. Try **Acapulco's** Mercado de Artesanías for handicrafts. Costera Alemán has air-conditioned malls.

TOURS AND EXCURSIONS

Puerto Vallarta: Bullfighting Wednesdays. Cruises, scuba diving, snorkelling and game fishing trips. Boat trips to inaccessible beaches. Details from Princess Bay Tours, tel and fax: (38) 26-0229, or hotel lobbies and travel agents.
Manzanillo: Sailing and game fishing excursions. November tournament. Snorkelling and scuba diving. Contact Underworld Scuba, tel: (333) 30642.
Ixtapa-Zihuatanejo: Scuba diving and snorkelling tours, tel: (755) 42147.

Acapulco: Boat trips around bay; scuba diving excursions; golf (three links); cruises. For trips down the Río Papagayo, contact **Shotover Jet**, Hotel Continental Plaza, Local 30, tel: (74) 84-1154.

USEFUL CONTACTS

US Consulates
Puerto Vallarta: Zaragoza 160, tel: (322) 20069.
Acapulco: Continental Plaza, La Costera, tel: (74) 81-1699.
UK Consulate
Acapulco: Hotel Las Brisas, Carretera Escénica 5255, tel: (74) 84-6605.
Golf Packages
Acapulco: Pierre Marquéz and Acapulco Princess, tel: 01-800-233-1818 (toll reduced); or Mayan Palace Golf Club, tel: (74) 66-1879.
Tourist Offices
Mazatlán: Av Camarón Sábalo, Calle Tiburón, tel: (69) 16-5160.
Puerto Vallarta: Palacio Municipal, Plaza Principal, tel: (322) 68080 ext 233.
Manzanillo: Blvd Miguel de la Madrid 4960, Playa Azul, tel: (333) 32277.
Ixtapa-Zihuatanejo: Alvarez, Zihuatanejo, tel: (755) 31967.
Acapulco: La Costera 4455, tel: (74) 81 1160.

ACAPULCO	J	F	M	A	M	J	J	A	S	O	N	D
AVERAGE TEMP. °F	80	80	80	80	83	83	83	84	83	83	82	81
AVERAGE TEMP. °C	26	26	26	26	28	28	28	29	28	28	28	27
RAINFALL in	0.3	-	-	-	1.5	10.9	11.1	8.7	15	6.2	1.3	0.4
RAINFALL mm	8	-	-	-	38	277	282	221	383	157	33	11

7
The Mayan Link

If Mexico is shaped like a traditional horn, the southern states represent a link between the main mass of Mexico to the north and the various countries of Central America to the south. It is a link in other ways, too, for this is the land of the Zapotecs and the Maya, whose territories extended through what is today Guatemala and Belize.

It is a small and relatively poor part of the country but culturally a very rich one, with colonial towns, a wealth of Indian handicrafts, impressive archaeological ruins and magnificent landscapes. The rugged Pacific coastline is likewise stunning, and several resorts have blossomed around Bahías de Huatalco, Puerto Ángel and Puerto Escondido. By contrast, the Gulf coast is rather flat and relatively uninteresting.

Long before today's visitors honed in on this particular part of Mexico, Oaxaca was home to the Zapotecs who built Monte Albán around 500BC. The Olmecs thrived in the area south of Villahermosa. Chiapas came under the influence of the Olmecs until 200BC, and later the Maya, who built the city states of Palenque, Yaxachilán and the smaller Toniná.

Hernán Cortés and the Spanish discovered Oaxaca in 1528 and such was his delight that Cortés declared himself Marqués del Valle de Oaxaca. Chiapas was, during Spanish rule, administered from Guatemala, and San Cristóbal de las Casas is a glorious mix of colonial Spain and earthy Indian. Don't expect Spanish to be the lingua franca here – any one of a dozen native languages is more often spoken in this area.

DON'T MISS

★★★ Oaxaca: a charming colonial town with myriad handicrafts.
★★★ Monte Albán: the remains of a Zapotec city from the first millennium.
★★★ Palenque: a ruined Mayan city in the jungle.
★★ Cañon de Sumidero: a deep-sided canyon in the tropical jungle.
★★ Voladores: extraordinary flying ritual at Papantla.

Opposite: *Rescued from the rampant jungle, the archaeological site at Palenque is one of the country's most impressive.*

CLIMATE

The geography of Mexico's southern states ranges from tropical coastline to mountains. On the coast and lowlands, temperatures are very **hot** and **humid** year-round. The higher the altitude, the more **moderate** the temperature, but there is high **rainfall** in the mountains and often **cold** winter weather, particularly at night.

HUATULCO

Strewn across rocky headlands and hidden behind sandy coves, Bahías de Huatulco is one of Mexico's newest and smartest resort areas. It melts into the tropical mountain foliage and looks out onto an endless stretch of unpolluted ocean. The nine bays with their 33 beaches along a 36km (22-mile) stretch of coast still make it easy to get away from the crowds, especially as some coves are only accessible from the sea. The attractions are, however, limited to the sea and beach, despite the construction of a number of luxury hotels and the golf course. In the heart of the area is the original village, **Santa Cruz Huatulco**, while a newer place, **La Crucecita**, has grown up at the junction of the coastal and inland roads. For those on a budget, these are alternative places to stay.

Favourite beaches include **Playa Santa Cruz** (the southern end is good for snorkelling over the coral reef, while boats depart for other beaches from the harbour), **San Agustín** for swimming and windsurfing, **La India**, a gorgeous, uncluttered bay further south, and **Tangounda**, the main beach north of Santa Cruz, in front of the major hotels and golf course. Recreation is in the form of swimming, snorkelling, diving, game fishing, jet ski trips, cruising and, inland, horseback riding and cycling.

OAXACA

Sitting on top of an arid plateau, Oaxaca successfully marries modernity with history. Though it has 250,000 inhabitants, it has a village-like intimacy. The Spanish settled around the *zócalo* in 1529 but it is the Indians, with their **colourful handicrafts**, that are more evident today. Their fabulous **Guelaguetza** festival of dance, held in July, is an Oaxacan highlight.

The *Zócalo* ★★

Starting point for exploring Oaxaca, the traffic-free **Alameda** and adjoining **Plaza de Armas** was the first area to be constructed by the Spanish. It is an ideal place to sit in one of the arcade cafés and soak up the atmosphere before a morning's sightseeing.

At the northern end stands the solid but uninspiring **Catedral**, begun in 1553 and finished some 200 years later. A superb example of Spanish Baroque is the **Iglesia de Santo Domingo**, located just a few blocks to the north, and also its new **Centro Cultural**, a fabulous museum where, among others, the treasures from Monte Albán's **Tomb 7** are housed. Other examples include the **Basílica de la Soledad** with its image of Oaxaca's patron saint, and the Baroque **Templo de San Felipe Neri**, where Oaxaca's most famous son, **Benito Juárez**, later president of Mexico, was married in 1843. A walk along the pedestrian **Calle Alcalá** allows you to admire the restored colonial buildings, now home to some of the town's best shops and restaurants.

Museum lovers will want to spend some time in the **Museo de Arte Contemporáneo** (containing works by Oaxaca-born Rufino Tamayo and other great local artists), take in the **Museo Regional de Oaxaca**, and perhaps admire the interesting archaeological exhibits in the **Museo Rufino Tamayo**.

Above: *Once a bandstand, this structure is now a café in the centre of the zócalo.*

Opposite: *Many Indians mix traditional costumes with modern clothing.*

Among surfers this is the place for waves. The '**Mexican Pipeline**' is the reason. The resort (its name means 'hidden port') is largely undeveloped (yet has all the basics) and still relies more on fishing as an industry than tourism. Swimmers head for **Puerto Angelito** where the waves are manageable and, if the winds are favourable, also to **Playas Marinero** and **Carrizalillo**. Inland, there are tours to two mangrove swamps in the neighbourhood. **Laguna de Manialtepec** and **Parque Nacional Lagunas de Chacahua** are both renowned for their prolific bird life. Best time to visit is mid-year in the mornings.

Above: *Monte Albán dates from the 6th century BC, although most of the ruins were originally constructed some 1500 years ago.*

Monte Albán ★★★

Dating from the 6th century BC, Monte Albán is a monumental epitaph to the Zapotec civilization that flourished for over a millennium and died out by the 8th century AD, when the Mixtecs took part of the city for themselves. Palaces, pyramid platforms, temples, tombs and homes were constructed in this town, and at its heyday (from around AD300–700) 25,000 citizens lived here.

Visitors can easily spend a whole day wandering around this impressive site surrounded by mountains. The **Gran Plaza**, centre of Monte Albán, and its arrow-shaped **Edificio J**, now believed to have been an observatory, are two focal points. There is also the **Juego de Pelota** ball court, and **Edificio L**, where huge slabs of carved stone, portraying what were thought to be dancers, were found.

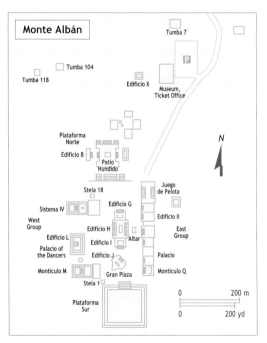

Mitla ★

Known as 'The Place of the Dead', this Zapotec ceremonial centre is some 45km (28 miles) southeast of Oaxaca. The ruins here mostly date from the 14th and 15th centuries. Some Mixtec pottery has been unearthed at the site, giving rise to the theory that the Mixtecs inhabited this region prior to a Zapotec reassertion and then the arrival of the Aztecs. The **Palace of the Columns** and the **Patio of Mosaics** are two of the highlights here.

TUXTLA GUTIÉRREZ

Capital of the province of Chiapas, Tuxtla Gutiérrez is not a city that entices tourists. It is, however, situated at a crossroads between the interior of Chiapas (and the town of San Cristóbal) and the capitals of its neighbouring states, Oaxaca and Tabasco. It is also well placed for a visit to the Sumidero Canyon, 18km (11 miles) to the north.

The town centres around **Plaza Cívica** and its snowy-white, modern **Catedral**, but the two main points of interest are located out of the centre. Devoted exclusively to Chiapas, the **Museo Regional de Chiapas** is a fascinating place for an insight into the culture of the area. Likewise, the oddly named **ZOOMAT**, an unusually fine zoo, is dedicated to Chiapas' rich fauna. Although most specimens are caged, the zoo has many free-ranging birds.

Cañon de Sumidero ★

Northeast of Tuxtla, slicing its way through the tropical mountains, lies the Sumidero Canyon. Vertically sided along its 15km (9.5-mile) length, this canyon has been carved out by the **Río Grande de Chiapas** (Río Grijalva). While not quite as breathtaking as Mexico's Copper Canyon (*see* pages 62 and 66), it is certainly impressive, and in parts it is over 1300m (4265ft) deep. The best way to see the canyon is by boat from **Chiapa de Corzo**, 17km (10.5 miles) east of Tuxtla, or at Cahuare, where the road to San Cristóbal crosses the river. Fast launches take tourists downriver through the canyon bristling with raccoons, butterflies, birds and crocodiles.

> ### SAN BARTOLO COYOTEPEC
>
> This village, 12km (7.5 miles) from Oaxaca, is renowned for its shiny black **pottery**. Known locally as **barro negro**, this black earthenware is actually a newish addition to the handicraft scene. It was started by **Rosa Nieto Real** in the 1960s and the tradition continues though she is no longer alive. The handmade pots are burnished prior to firing and turn black because of mineral oxides in the clay and because the kilns are closed and keep in the dark wood smoke. Frequent buses run to the village from central Oaxaca. Afternoons are the best time to visit.

Below left: *The massive cliffs of the awe-inspiring Sumidero Canyon.*

> ### A LEAP INTO THE VOID
>
> **Chiapa de Corzo**, situated just 10km (6 miles) from Tuxtla Gutiérrez, was founded in 1528 by **Captain Diego de Mazariegos**. He chose a site along the banks of the **Río Grijalva** where the **Chiapa tribe** were living. Fiercely proud and preferring an honourable death to a life of slavery under the Spanish, the Chiapas – men, women and children – chose to commit **suicide** by jumping from the 1000m (3281ft) sheer cliffs into the **Sumidero Canyon**.

LAGUNAS DE MONTEBELLO

The first nature reserve to be created in the state of Chiapas was the **Parque Nacional Lagunas de Montebello**, to protect the Montebello and other lagoons in the Comitán area, near the Guatemala border. This beautiful region covers over 7000ha (17,297 acres) and comprises some 59 **lakes** and **lagoons**. Among the flora are a large variety of **orchids** and **ferns**. The Parque also has some **Mayan ruins** and a series of **multicoloured lakes** – each of the five lakes is quite a different colour.

Below right: *Like the town, the Cathedral of San Cristóbal de las Casas is unusually colourful.*

BACKSTRAP LOOM

The most widespread method of **weaving** in Mexico is the backstrap loom. Easy to use, portable and inexpensive to make, the loom is constructed out of **bamboo** or **wood**. One end of the loom is tied to a post or tree, and the other end, a **broad band** linking either side of the loom, is looped behind the weaver's back. Leaning backwards, she can maintain a **taut working surface** as she sends the shuttle with the weft thread back and forth through the warp threads that form the length of the fabric.

San Cristóbal de las Casas ★★

It is hard not to fall for this provincial town. Small enough to walk around, colourful with its Indian population and historic in its colonial architecture, San Cristóbal lies in a high-level valley, just 83km (52 miles) from Tuxtla, and is surrounded by pine-clad mountains.

Plaza 31 de Marzo is the social centre of town and a good spot to get a feel for San Cristóbal. Cafés abound. The ochre and maroon **Catedral** on the north side, rebuilt in 1693, has a glorious golden interior. **Templo de Santo Domingo** is arguably the most beautiful church in town.

The **Mercado Municipal**, eight blocks to the north, and the **Mercado de Artesanías** in Plaza Santo Domingo offer a flamboyant display of Indian cultures, specifically those of the Huastecs, Chamula and Zinacantecans, and the differences between these various cultures soon become apparent. On sale are livestock, herbs, handicrafts and flowers. This is also the place to buy fabulous *huipiles* (embroidered blouses), shawls, belts and bags.

A visit to **Na Balom** (Jaguar House) is fascinating. Housed in an old seminary, this museum-cum-hotel was owned by archaeologist Frans Blom and his anthropologist wife Gertrude, who befriended the local Lacandòn Indians and brought to light much about their culture.

Excursions to local villages include the Sunday markets in **San Juan Chamula** (visit the church with its extraordinary semipagan rituals), **Zinacantán** or **Tenejapa**.

Palenque

Around the time Europeans were struggling with the technique of producing a simple arch, the Maya, under their king, Pakal (AD615–683), were flourishing in the city of Palenque, an urban complex that covered nearly 65km² (25 sq miles) in the midst of a verdant, lowland jungle. Excavations reveal that the site was inhabited from the 1st century AD.

Above: *The ancient eight-storey Templo de las Inscripciones, Palenque, is the burial place of Pakal.*

Palenque (not to be confused with the modern town just a few kilometres away) is a vast archaeological site with some exquisite Mayan stone decoration. It is, for some, the most mysterious of Mesoamerican cities and seeing it in the early morning, when wisps of light mist linger amongst the dense tropical rain forest, and monkeys and parrots cavort through the canopy, it is easy to see why. Although the stone today is a weathered grey, the buildings were originally painted red.

In 1952 archaeologists opened Pakal's tomb in the eight-storey **Temple of the Inscriptions** and found his skeleton and a **death mask** of jade, obsidian and shell. **El Palacio**, **Templo del Sol** (the views are good from its summit), **Templo del Jaguar** and the **Grupo de la Cruz** give further perspective to this formerly great city.

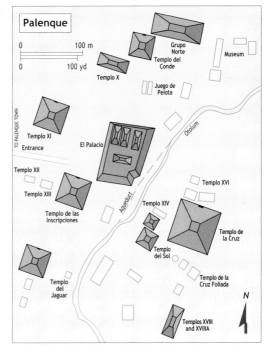

Palenque

0   100 m

0   100 yd

Grupo Norte
Museum
Templo del Conde
Templo X
Juego de Pelota
TO PALENQUE TOWN
Templo XI
Entrance
El Palacio
Otolúm
Templo XII
Templo XVI
Templo XIII
Templo de las Inscripciones
Aqueduct
Templo XIV
Templo de la Cruz
Templo del Sol
Templo del Jaguar
Templo de la Cruz Foliada
N
Templos XVIII and XVIIIA

Villahermosa ★

For many visitors the starting (or finishing) point for a visit to Palenque, this tropical city is not a major stop for the culture-hungry traveller. However, thanks to oil reserves, the town is a pleasant one and it does have the best collection of **Olmec art**. **Parque Museo La Venta** is an open-air archaeological museum, while the **Museo Regional de Antropología** is linked with the **Centro de Investigaciones de las Culturas Olmeca y Maya**, also known as the CICOM, a research institute dedicated to the Olmec and Mayan cultures.

Above: *This enormous Olmec head can be seen in Villahermosa.*
Opposite: *Unwinding slowly from their pole, the voladores of Papantla slowly rotate until they reach ground level.*

THE GULF COAST

Less visited than other areas, this coast and its hinterland have a handful of interesting sights.

Veracruz ★★

Veracruz was Cortés' first landing point in Mexico and it has remained an important port ever since, despite being occupied for short periods by both French and US troops.

What Veracruz lacks in monuments it makes up for in atmosphere. A vibrant, party-loving city, it blossoms to the sound of Mariachi and marimba music, reaching a heady boiling point during **Carnaval**. The **Plaza de Armas** (*zócalo*) is the pulse of the city and a good place to enjoy a drink under one of the porticos. The **cathedral** is on the south, the **Palacio Municipal** on the east, and the **malécon** just behind. The only surviving bastion from the city wall (there used to be nine), **Baluarte de Santiago**, dates from 1526 and is open to the public; there is a small museum inside. Offshore, though linked by a causeway, the **Castillo de San Juan de Ulúa** is a fortress and sometime prison built on a coral reef.

If you don't plan on diving off Veracruz, take time to visit the **acuario**, a fine aquarium full of the local fauna.

Catemaco ★

Located on the shores of Lake Catemaco and amid a lovely landscape, this pleasant town is best known for its *brujos*, or **witch doctors**. Other diversions include a trip to one of the lake's islands, **Isla de los Monos**, where a colony of monkeys, originally from Thailand, belongs to the University of Veracruz.

Jalapa ★

Archaeology buffs head straight for the **Museo de Antropología de Jalapa** for its marvellous collection of Olmec artefacts set in a fine modern museum. Dating from the period 1200–900BC, the museum's seven massive stone heads are testament to the creativity of a great civilization. An excursion to **Hacienda Lencero**, a country estate turned museum, is also of interest.

Papantla ★★

The commercial backbone of Papantla is vanilla, but it is its famous *voladores*, or flyers, that pack in the crowds. These seemingly fearless flyers launch themselves, four at a time, from the top of a pole and, having previously twisted their lifelines around the pole, hang upside down as they gently unwind to touch the ground.

El Tajín ★

One of the most important archaeological sites in the country, El Tajín was occupied by the Totonacs from around AD100–1200, though the ruins that we see today are believed to date from AD600–700 and show signs of influence by other great civilizations. The seven-storey **Pirámide de los Nichos**, with its 365 deep-set niches (a stone calendar of sorts), is an impressive structure quite unlike other ancient pyramids. The Ball Court, **Juego de Pelota Sur**, is remarkable mainly for its sculptured panels depicting rituals associated with the game.

VOLADORES

The origin of this ceremony is unsure despite representations found on **Totonac reliefs**. Some say it is a **fertility rite**, others see **numerical links** with the number of days and weeks in a year. Today the ritual has **commercial value**. The four voladores and their musician perform each weekend and during the Feast of **Corpus Christi**. They also perform, for a fee, a number of times a week at **El Tajín** and several times a day in front of the **Museo de Antropología** in Mexico City.

The Mayan Link at a Glance

The drier winter months, **Nov** to **Apr** are best. However, annual festivals (Guelaguetza in July, Posadas in December in Oaxaca; and Semana Santa in San Cristóbal) attract travellers, so at these times book in advance.

Huatulco, Villahermosa, Oaxaca and Veracruz all have **airports**. **Buses** between the major destinations are frequent, but not particularly fast, and available in first and second class from their respective bus stations. Avoid travel at night in the highlands: the hairpin bends are dangerous enough. **Train** services are presently suspended, but a precision railroad system is planned.

Buses and taxis are available in the main towns. But it is simple to get around by foot in the heart of Veracruz, Villahermosa, Oaxaca and San Cristóbal.

LUXURY

Quinta Real, 4 Blvd Benito Juárez, Tangolunda, Huatulco, tel: (958) 10428, fax: 10429. Small, beautiful all-suite hotel.
Hotel Camino Real, 5 de Mayo 300, Oaxaca, tel: (951) 60611, fax: 60732. A 16th-century convent, prison and now an ultra-luxurious hotel with excellent restaurant.

Camino Real Tuxtla Gutiérrez, Blvd Domínguez 1195, Tuxtla Gutiérrez, tel: (961) 77777, fax: 77799. Comfortable modern hotel, slightly out of centre.
Hyatt Regency Villahermosa, Calle Juárez, Colonia Linda-vista, Villahermosa, tel: (93) 15-1234, fax: 15-5808. Fairly central, large and luxurious.
Fiesta Americana, Blvd Avila Camacho, Veracruz, tel: (29) 89-8989, fax: 89-8904. Modern, state-of-the-art comfort in the seafront.

MID-RANGE

Hotel Flamboyant, Plaza Principal, La Crucecita, Huatulco, tel: (958) 70105, fax: 70121. Pretty hotel, good position with pool.
Hotel Monte Albán, Alameda de León 1, Oaxaca, tel: (951) 62777, fax: 63265. Clean and very central.
Hotel María Eugenia, Av Central Ote 507 at 4 Ote, Tuxtla Gutiérrez, tel: (961) 33767, fax: 32860. Decent, centrally located hotel with good restaurant.
Hotel Casa Mexicana, 28 de Agosto, San Cristóbal de las Casas, tel: (967) 80683, fax: 82627. Pretty hotel with interesting art and furniture, well situated. Good restaurant.
Hotel Tulija Days, Carretera a las Ruinas, Palenque, tel: (934) 50104, fax: 50163. Tranquil hotel, tropical gardens, good restaurant and pool slightly out of town centre.

Howard Johnson Hotel, Aldama 404, Villahermosa, tel and fax: (93) 14-4645. Modern hotel in centre of Zona Luz.
Hotel Emporio, Paseo del Malécon 210, Veracruz, tel: (29) 32-0020, fax: 31-2261. Harbour views, comfortable rooms and centrally situated.
Hotel Xalapa, Victoria, Jalapa, tel and fax: (28) 12-7920. Modern, clean and pleasant with pool.

BUDGET

Hotel Soraya, Playa Principal, Puerto Ángel, tel: (958) 43009. Small hotel, centrally located. Excellent value.
Posada del Parque, Flamboyán 16, La Crucecita, Huatulco, tel: (958) 70219. Well placed on the plaza.
Hotel Principal, 5 de Mayo 208, Oaxaca, tel and fax: (951) 62535. Small, central, ever-popular. Booking essential.
Hotel Fray Bartolomé de las Casas, Niños Heroes & Insurgentes 2, San Cristóbal de las Casas, tel: (967) 80932, fax: 83510. Popular, friendly, colonial building turned hotel.
Hotel Maya Tulipanes, Calle Cañada 6, Palenque Town, tel: (934) 50201, fax: 51004. Friendly, garden hotel.
Hotel Miraflores, Reforma 304, Villahermosa, tel: (93) 12-0022, fax: 12-0486. Quiet, good location in Zona Luz.
Hotel Imperial, Zócalo, Veracruz, tel: (29) 321204. Old-world ambience, clean, friendly, very central location.

The Mayan Link at a Glance

Hotel María Victoria, Zaragoza 6, Jalapa, tel: (28) 17-3530. Small, clean hotel with good restaurant.

LUXURY

Las Cupulas Restaurant, Hotel Quinta Real, Huatulco (*see* Where to Stay). Smart dining, great ambience. Mexican and international cuisine.

El Refectorio, Hotel Camino Real, Oaxaca (*see* Where to Stay). Serves excellent Mexican, Oaxacan and international dishes.

Hotel Hyatt Regency Villahermosa restaurants, Villahermosa (*see* Where to Stay). Mexican and international cuisine.

MID-RANGE

Sabor de Oaxaca, La Crucecita, Huatulco. This very popular restaurant serves Oaxacan cuisine.

El Naranjo, Trujana 203, Oaxaca, tel: (951) 41878. Central, excellent Oaxacan specialities.

Hosteria de Alcala, Alcala 307, tel: (951) 62093. Nicely decorated patio including a fountain; Typical Oaxacan and international cuisine.

Restaurant Las Pichanchas, Av Central Ote 837, Tuxtla Gutiérrez, tel: (961) 25351. Good regional cuisine, music.

El Fogón de Jovel, Av 16 de Septiembre 11, San Cristóbal de las Casas, tel: (967) 81153. Fine regional cuisine in lovely courtyard setting.

La Parilla, Av Belisario Dominguez, San Cristóbal de las Casas, tel: (967) 85738. Excellent grilled meat.

Pardiños, Landero and Cos 146, Veracruz, tel: (29) 31-7571. Seafood, Jarochos and international cuisine.

Café de la Parroquia has two sites on the Malecon, in downtown Veracruz, tel: (29) 32 1855. The oldest café in Veracruz, good Mexican cuisine.

La Pergola, Jalapa. Outside dining, good Mexican cuisine.

BUDGET

Los Portales, Calle Bugambilia, La Crucecita, Huatulco. Popular restaurant, good tacos and Mexican food.

Restaurant Maya, corner of Independencía and Hidalgo, Palenque. Popular set menus.

In **Huatulco** you will find Mercado Central, La Crucecita. There are also hotel shops.
Oaxaca is a shopper's paradise. Shops offer quality; markets offer inexpensive prices. There is black **pottery** from San Bartolo Coyotepec, rugs, *huipiles* from Oaxaca and Chiapas, colourful carved animals, jewellery and leather goods. Try the **Central de Abastos**, for variety of goods, and the **Mercado de Artesanías** has a large selection of Indian crafts and handiwork.

Huatulco: Bike and other eco tours, **Rent a Bike**, tel: (958) 70669; horseback riding tours. Agencia de Viajes Paraíso Huatulco, tel: (958) 10055, for tours around Huatulco and further afield. Scuba diving, **Buceos Sotaventos**, tel: (958) 10051.
Tuxtla Gutiérrez: Kali Tours, Hotel María Eugenia (*see* Where to Stay), tel: (961) 13175. Tours to Sumidero Canyon and other excellent sights.

Tourist Offices
Oaxaca: Independencia 607, tel: (951) 47788, and 5 de Mayo 200, tel: (951) 64828.
San Cristóbal de las Casas: Palacio Municipal, tel: (967) 86570.
Palenque (town): Mercado de Artesanías on Juárez, tel: (934) 50356.
Villahermosa: Paseo Tabasco 1504, Tabasco 2000, tel: (93) 16-5143.
Veracruz: Palacio Municipal, tel: (29) 89 8817.
Jalapa: entrance of the Palacio Municipal, tel: (28) 42 1214.

OAXACA	J	F	M	A	M	J	J	A	S	O	N	D
AVERAGE TEMP. °F	57	62	67	73	78	81	79	82	78	72	63	59
AVERAGE TEMP. °C	14	17	19	23	26	27	26	28	26	22	17	15
RAINFALL in	0.5	1	1	1	1.5	3	2.5	2.5	5	3	1.5	1
RAINFALL mm	13	24	25	33	35	76	58	61	115	75	38	25

8
Yucatán

Ancient ruins swamped by thick jungle, limpid waters with myriad fish, dazzling white beaches and unique wildlife reserves – this is the Yucatán Peninsula. An area of predominantly flat limestone with over 1250km (about 777 miles) of coastline, the Yucatán comprises three states: Campeche, Yucatán and Quintana Roo. Colonial **Mérida** was historically its busiest city but today, with the vast resort developments on the eastern shores of the peninsula, Cancún has become the most important city. Cancún is the mecca for sun-seekers but Playa del Carmen, just 68km (42 miles) to the south down what is now known as the **Riviera Maya**, is challenging its role with a gentler style of tourism and better beaches.

Nearby, the beautiful island of Cozumel offers yet another facet of resort living. Tempered by the crystal-clear waters surrounding it and the fishing community which lives there, Cozumel has its own adherents, many of whom are divers.

But despite the numerous resorts, the Yucatán is not only about modern man. It was an important stronghold of the ancient Maya. As you sail off the eastern shores you can look back, much as those Maya did, and gaze on the ruins of Tulum, also known as the City of the Dawn. Inland, the ruins of Cobá, Izamal, Kabah, Uxmal and huge Chichén Itzá have all been reclaimed from the lush tropical forests. Nowhere else in Mexico do pre-history and the present rub shoulders quite as closely as they do in the Yucatán.

DON'T MISS

*** **Chichén Itzá:** one of the Maya's greatest cities.
*** **Cozumel:** world-class snorkelling and diving.
** **Mérida:** a lovely colonial town, capital of the Yucatán.
** **Uxmal:** another great Mayan city in the Puuc Hills.
** **Tulum:** a Mayan city perfectly perched on the edge of the ocean.
** **Dolphins:** swim with them in Xel-Há, Chankanaab, or off Isla Mujeres.
** **Sian Ka'an Biosphere:** one of the country's prime nature reserves.

Opposite: *The Caribbean and the tropical climate bring tourists to Cancún.*

CLIMATE

The tropical interior is **hot** and **humid** throughout the year. **Rainfall** is heaviest from April–May and from September–January. The average daytime summer temperature is 34°C (93°C), and it drops to only a few degrees lower in other seasons. The weather in **November** to **April** is generally **balmy**, with lower humidity and cooling breezes. The Yucatán Peninsula is sometimes affected by **hurricanes** that blow in from the Gulf of Mexico or the Caribbean, usually between **July** and **October**.

Below: *A section of the baluarte (fortifications) in central Campeche.*

CAMPECHE

Although Campeche was a Mayan stronghold when the Spanish landed, it was fishing and then oil that changed its profile, and today most people are involved, in some way, in these industries. It is not a place that features highly on tourist itineraries but it is a very pleasant colonial seaside town, with good seafood and impressive *baluarte* (fortresses), which deserves better publicity.

Seven of the original eight bulwarks still stand and it is worth a stroll to see **Baluarte de San Carlos** (inside there are dungeons and models of the original fortifications) and **Baluarte de la Soledad** (which houses the Museo de Estelas Maya). Two blocks south from the seaside *malecón* is the **Parque Principal** (Plaza de la Independencia), the soul of the city. Shady trees encourage locals to linger. The Baroque **Catedral** is on the east side, and the arcaded **Palacio de Gobierno** two blocks to the west. Delightful domestic architecture is also there for the discovering. Wander down Calle 55 to visit the **Casa de Artesanías** and you will come across a number of elegant homes.

Campeche is an excellent jumping-off point for visits to the archaeological sites at **Edzná** and, further away, those at **Uxmal**, **Kabah** and **Sayil**.

Uxmal ★★

Dating back to the late Classical period, this is one of the best Mayan cities discovered in the Puuc Hills. Attractions include the large quadrangles, such as the one in the centre of **La Monjas** (the Nunnery, now thought to be a misnomer), with its stone mosaics and geometric designs sculpted in limestone, and the **Palacio del Gobernador** with its stone mosaic frieze. Look out for the turtles on the cornice of the **Casa de las Tortugas**. The **Juego de Pelota** (ball court) encloses a court 34m (37yd) long by 10m (11yd) wide. The nightly *Son et Lumière* performance is a great way to get a feel for this ruined city.

Left: *Not very often visited, Kabah provides an insight into the lives of small-town Maya.*

CENOTES

The **Maya** focused much of their culture around **water** despite, or perhaps because of, the lack of water in the Yucatán. Rain was the basis for survival, and the **water god** was the most often represented deity in temples. The Maya took advantage of caves and *cenotes* – **underground rivers** or **sinkholes**. More than 440 cenotes have been discovered in the Yucatán and these are becoming increasingly popular places to visit for both nature lovers and scuba divers. **Dzitnup**, near Valladolid, is perhaps the best known.

Other Mayan Cities ★

South of Uxmal are the ruins of **Sayil**, **Xlapak**, **Labná** and **Kabah**. Sayil thrived late in the Classical period, coming to an end around AD1000. The most interesting structure here is the three-level **Palacio**, built on top of a hill. Xlapak is noted for its small yet heavily decorated **Palacio**. Labná is known mainly for its finely ornamented arch, an imposing entrance to an area presumed to have been used for important celebrations. The wealth of detail is highly impressive. There is also the **Mirador** and, attached by a *sacbe* stone causeway, the **Palacio**.

Kabah is one of the best examples of the Puuc style of architecture. Stop in front of the **Codz Poop** (Palace of Masks) with its hundreds of masks of Chac Mool, the Mayan rain god, or walk outside the **Palacio** and admire the creativity of artists who lived over 1000 years ago. The Codz Poop is unique in its undulating design and it is worth a journey just to see it.

Yucatán Peninsula

0 100 km
0 60 miles

Parque Nacional Río Lagartos · Isla Mujeres · Cancún · Río · Parque Nacional Lagartos · San Felipe · Tizimín · Culuba · Progreso · Ekbalám · Playa del Carmen · Ria Celestún · Parque Natural · Mérida · Motul · Valladolid · Cobá · Celestún · Cozumel · La Costa · Chichén Itzá · Tulum · Isla · Uxmal · Kabah · Peto · Muyil · Chamax · Jaina · Uxmal · Sayil · Labná · Vigía Chico · Punta Allen · Xtacumbilxunán · Campeche · Felipe Carrillo · Edzná · Xmaben · Naranjal · Puerto · Champotón · Xochob · Sian Ka'an Biosphere Reserve · Sabancuy · Pustunich · Becan · Majahual · Isla del Carmen · Puerto Real · Chicaná · Xpujil · Calderitas · Chetumal · Banco Chinchorro · Ciudad del Carmen · Escárcega · Xpujil · Kohunlich · Xcalac · Santa Cecilia · Candelaria · Calakmul · Walk · Orange · Ambergris Cay · Ciudad Pemex · El Triunfo · Nuevo Coahuila · La Unión · Hicks Cays · GUATEMALA · BELIZE

Above: *The morning flag ceremony in Mérida.*
Opposite: *The pyramid of El Castillo, Chichén Itzá.*

THE HACIENDA TRAIL

In the 17th century, many of the wealthy elite constructed **working haciendas** for the cultivation of **sisal** around **Mérida**. Over 362 were built, of which 71 still have their original architectural details. With exotic Mayan or evocative colonial names, they are a wonderful **historical heritage**. Some have been converted into hotels, others are open to the public and offer a glimpse into a gracious lifestyle of another era.

MÉRIDA

Capital of the state of Yucatán, Mérida is a very pleasant and clean colonial city. It was founded in 1542 on the site of a former Mayan city, Ichcaanziho, and named after the Spanish town in which Hernán Cortés, and other conquistadors, were born.

The focal point of the city is, as it was in Mayan times, the large, shady *zócalo*, or **Plaza Mayor**. Here is situated the massive 16th-century **cathedral** which tactlessly incorporated some of the stones from the Mayan temple. The **Palacio Municipal**, opposite, is an evening venue for Yucatecan dances; the colonial **Palacio de Gobierno** houses some spectacular and moving murals by Pacheco depicting the history of the Maya and the Spanish; **Casa Montejo**, formerly owned by the conquering Montejo family, is now a bank; and the **Museo de Arte Contemporáneo** (MAKAY) is the city's modern art museum, housed in a colonial seminary.

Mérida's answer to the Paseo de la Reforma is the green and airy **Paseo de Montejo**. The **Museo Regional de Antropología** on this Paseo is a fine place to get an overall perspective of Yucatán and, in particular, Mayan culture. Lastly, look around the **Mercado Municipal**. This, and the surrounding area, is the place to buy cotton clothing, Mexican hammocks and *jipijapa* (panama hats).

Keen divers head northwards to the **Alcranes Reef**, 120km (75 miles) off the coast. An undisturbed island, it has excellent flora and fauna.

CHICHÉN ITZÁ

During the European Dark Ages, man strove to survive. In the Yucatán, at the same time, man was thriving – studying the stars, creating a calendar and producing great cities such as Chichén Itzá.

Between AD500 and 1200, the Maya build this vast centre which, although it incorporates several other Mesoamerican cultural elements, is the most complete ruined Mayan city in the entire Yucatán Peninsula. It was a ceremonial and commercial centre where hundreds of people lived.

One of the highlights of this magnificent 15km² (6 sq mile) site is **El Castillo**, a beautifully proportioned pyramid crowned by a temple dedicated to the cult of **Kukulcán**, the Mayan serpent god. This pyramid is also thought to have had something to do with the Mayan calendar, for it has exactly 365 steps, a 45-degree stair-case and nine levels. During both the equinoxes, the play of light and shadow on the staircases simulates a serpent in descent.

The **Juego de Pelota**, the largest in Mesoamerica, was the scene of *pelota* (ball) games at the end of which the losers were actually sacrificed. The **Cenote de los Sacrificios** was where this all happened, although archaeologists have revealed that the sick and elderly, too, met their end here. Other interesting sights to visit at Chichén Itzá include the **Templo de los Jaguares**, the **Templo de los Guerreros** with its attractive **Mil Columnas** (rows of tall white columns), the round **Observatorio** (one of the few circular buildings built by the Maya), and the **Casa de las Águilas**.

IZAMAL

Another colonial town built on Mayan soil, Izamal is particularly well known for its impressive **Convento de San Antonio de Padua**, constructed in 1553 on top of the destroyed Mayan temple, **Popul-Chac**. It was designed as a vast Franciscan monastery whose enormous atrium rivalled in size that of St Peter's, Rome.

Opposite: *Moped and car rental is quite easy in Cancún as the traffic here is not too hectic.*
Below: *Chac Mool, the Mayan god of rain, presides over the white sandy beach and the blue ocean at the resort of Cancún.*

CANCÚN

Cancún has neither Mayan ruins nor a colonial legacy. Thirty years ago Cancún was a small village nestling behind a dazzlingly white sandbar. With the rise of mass tourism, Mexico's tourism authority saw the potential and a resort began to take shape. Today, Cancún (the town) is an orderly urban development to the north of the resort area, which is linked to the **Hotel Zone**. This erstwhile sandbar is flanked on one side by the Caribbean and on the other by **Nichupté Lagoon**. Here, for over 15km (9 miles) along the **Paseo Kukulcán**, is a cornucopia of luxury hotels, ending where a bridge takes the road back inland to the nearby international airport. It is a beautifully manicured but expensive resort that has been geared towards North Americans and their requirements. The easiest way to afford a stay here is on a package tour available through Mexicana Airlines.

The best of Cancún is the cool, dazzlingly white beach (the 'sand' is actually made up of broken fossils) and its range of watersports. This is the place to be pampered in a luxury hotel, take a cruise, relax around a free-form pool or float in the limpid turquoise shallows, play a round of **golf** (two courses are open to nonresidents) or a few sets of **tennis**, and then to party all night long. In the numerous shopping plazas – such as **Caracol**, **La Fiesta**, **Kukulcán** or **Flamingo** – are **smart shops** and **boutiques** (or the **Ki Huic** artisans' market located in Cancún Town), restaurants suitable for all tastes (though usually for the fatter variety of wallets), and also plenty of pulsating nightlife.

The best **watersports** along the Hotel Zone are operated by **AquaWorld** and include snorkelling and diving (though the diving is much better off the Cozumel reefs), kayaking, parasailing, and riding water scooters.

It would, however, be a pity to miss the hinterland, for Cancún is very well placed to visit **Río Lagartos Biosphere Reserve** and its 25,000 pink flamingos, the Mayan ruins at **Chichén Itzá** (see page 111), as well as all the attractions on the south coast.

Isla Mujeres ★★

Once the haunt of backpacking cognoscenti, Isla Mujeres (Island of Women) is now becoming a popular resort island with visitors looking for less razzle and more relaxation. Once inhabited by a few Maya (there is a small ruin of a **temple**), the island is only about 8km (5 miles) long, just 11km (7 miles) offshore, and easy to get around either by foot or by moped. Although the 'town' is in the northern part and has beaches, the western (sheltered) and southern shores are the best places for **swimming**, **snorkelling** and beachcombing.

Some 25km (15 miles) north of Isla Mujeres and accessible from the island (or from Cancún), **Isla Contoy** is another special biosphere reserve where waterbirds breed.

DESAYUNO, YUCATÁN STYLE

A traditional Yucatán **breakfast** consists of fried eggs served on a crispy tortilla and usually accompanied by ham, tomatoes, onions and beans, all doused in a spicy chilli sauce.

PLAYA DEL CARMEN

This village was virtually unknown 20 years ago. It was – and is – the departure point for ferries to **Cozumel** but development has turned it into a ribbon-like resort which continues to grow luxury hotels southwards, absorbing the pristine beaches along the Caribbean shore.

Playa del Carmen is less brash than Cancún and has great beaches (arguably even better ones than Cozumel), particularly south towards **Akumal** and **Tulum**.

Regular transport up and down the coast (the **Riviera Maya**) between Cancún, just 68km (42 miles) to the north, and **Boca Paila**, some 92km (57 miles) south, means that beaches, Mayan villages, natural reserves and archaeological sites are easily accessible.

Cozumel protects Playa's shores, so watersports are safe here. **Swimming**, **body surfing**, **snorkelling**, **game fishing** and **diving** are all popular. Then there are good **restaurants** (especially along the pedestrians-only **Avenida Quinta**) and bars, some smart shops, and many upmarket hotels in the newer Hotel Zone.

From Playa to Punta Allen there are a number of interesting places to visit and there are plenty of tours to take you there if you don't want to hire a car or catch a bus. **Xcaret**, **Puerto Aventuras**, **Xel-Há** (see page 118) or the **Sian Ka'an Biosphere Reserve** (see page 119) are quite easily accessible, as are the archaeological sites of **Cobá** and **Tulum**.

Cobá ★

It takes only a couple of hours to reach inland Cobá from Playa, and not much longer by the motorway from Cancún. This was one of the Maya's largest settlements and was built before Chichén Itzá or Tulum. Its heyday was from AD600–900 and the city is thought to have extended over 70km² (27 sq miles), housing some 40,000 inhabitants. Unlike Tulum and Chichén Itzá, it sees relatively few tourists.

Archaeologists believe that over 6000 buildings were constructed here (the majority still hidden by the jungle), though the style is varied and shows a number of influences from Tikal (Guatemala). Most puzzling are the *sacbe*, or **stone causeways**, which radiate out from Cobá, the longest running an extraordinary 100km (62 miles) to the Mayan settlement of Yaxuna.

The major attraction here is the great pyramid of **Nohoch Mul**, which pierces the jungle canopy and affords magnificent panoramas from its summit. In the Macanxoc group there are beautiful **stelae** (stone tablets) to see, also **statues** of some of the queens from Tikal.

Above: *Playa del Carmen provides a less glitzy, generally more laid-back atmosphere than Cancún.*
Below: *Pausing for a moment of reflection at Cobá.*

COZUMEL

Hernán Cortés first landed in Mexico at Cozumel, the
country's largest island, just 20km (12 miles) from Playa
del Carmen. Measuring just 50 by 18km (31 by 11
miles), Cozumel remains largely undeveloped, despite its
appeal to tourists and cruise ships. It has fabulous reefs,
tepid waters and good beaches, though the pounding
surf on the east coast prohibits extensive swimming.

Records show that the **Maya** visited Cozumel as
early as AD300, venerating their goddess of fertility,
Ixchel. Then, in the 17th century, pirates lay low on the
island. When **Jacques Cousteau** proclaimed Cozumel's
underwater beauty, the island gained international
fame. Palancar Reef, the second-longest in the world, is
known to scuba divers worldwide.

Getting around Cozumel is easy enough. Roads are
paved and transport is by hired car, jeep, moped or
taxi. Some of the less crowded beaches, such as Playa
Bonita, are accessible only by jeep. **San Miguel** is small
enough to explore on foot. Here are some hotels,
restaurants and dozens of duty-free shops.

One of the highlights is a visit to the **Parque Nacional
Chankanaab**, on the bay of the same name just 9km (5.5
miles) south of San Miguel. This is a botanical garden

and a superb hands-on underwater reserve where you can snorkel with the friendly fish, **swim with dolphins** (for a fee), and see almost as many reef fish as you might on a dive trip. The gardens, too, are magnificent.

El Cedral, the site of a Mayan ruin (not in very good condition), is the venue for a local fiesta that takes place in May each year. The lighthouse at **Punta Celarain** affords great views across the island. Turtles are the main reason for a trip to **Playa Chen Río**: these amphibians frequent much of the eastern shores of Quintana Roo, lumbering ashore to lay their eggs, and here Cozumel is doing much to protect them.

> **DIVING FUN**
>
> Many hotels run introductory or **resort courses** where, under strict supervision, **novices** can dive in waters with temperatures that rarely drop below 27°C (81°F), pick up a few of the practical basics, and see some of the myriad **flora** and **fauna** that make the **coral reefs** so exciting. Then, if time permits, a full **certificate course** can be completed in four or five days.

Scuba Diving ★★★

The **Palancar Reef** extends over 37km (23 miles) offshore from Cozumel. It boasts over 200 species of tropical fish, black coral, underwater caves and tunnels and, unusually, an aircraft wreck. To enjoy some of these wonders – and they are breathtaking – it is not essential to have a PADI or NAUI dive certificate. Dive operations will teach you on the spot and are, in some cases, happy to take along snorkellers, particularly to shallower sites on the Palancar and Colombia reefs. Advanced divers head offshore for the **Maracaibo**, **Paraíso** and **Yocab** reefs where, drifting along with the welling currents, they will get to see more pelagic fish. Almost all diving here is drift diving in light currents. Those who don't want to get wet can take glass-bottom boat rides over the reef.

Opposite: *Chankanaab, one of Cozumel's easy snorkelling spots on an island famed for its diving.*

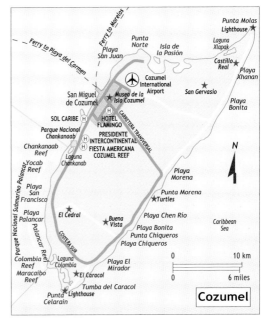

Cozumel

OTHER SIGHTS

The exquisite coast and its myriad beaches, from Playa del Carmen down to the Belize border, is now the focus of further resort development. There are individual resorts along many of the most beautiful bays, and several others are in the pipeline.

Xcaret has been transformed into an eco-archaeological theme park, where visitors can swim with the tropical fish and dolphins, take rides through the underground tunnels, and discover (in the aviary) some of the regional birds which used to fly free. There are a couple of Mayan ruins which have been restored and, to complete the picture, there is an evening show called **Xcaret Nights** which offers cameos of Mayan and Mexican culture through dance and music.

Above right and below:

The stunning lagoon at Xel-Há forms part of an ecological theme park where you can snorkel with tropical fish or, as below, swim with the dolphins.

Further south on the road to Tulum, passing through **Xpu-Há Ecopark**, **Paamal** with its lagoons, the large resort area of **Puerto Aventuras**, and the beautiful, broad bay at **Akumal** (now largely developed), the road reaches the small ruins of **Xel-Há**. Most people, however, come in busloads to swim in the gorgeous lagoon amid the tropical fish. Best times to visit are before or after the bus trips when the lagoon is tranquil. The highlight here is the chance to pet dolphins for a fee.

Tulum ★★

Just 68km (42 miles) south of Playa, Tulum sits atop a cliff facing the endless miles of turquoise Caribbean Sea. It is a magnificent site for a Mayan fishing port, albeit it one with Toltec influences, and one that was still occupied when the Spanish disembarked. The highlights in this fortified town include **El Castillo** (the watchtower) with its frieze, the two-storey **El Templo de los Frescos**, with the remains of three levels of frescoes (look at the wonderful head-dresses), and **El Templo del Dios Descendente**.

Sian Ka'an Biosphere Reserve ★★

Another 50km (31 miles) down the increasingly developed road, is the turn-off for Sian Ka'an, one of Mexico's finest reserves. It comprises one-third tropical forest, one-third marshland and one-third coast. Trips take visitors through the area by boat where they can observe egrets, kingfishers, frigate birds, herons and rare storks. There are also pumas, jaguars and crocodiles, and, in the lagoon, turtles and a fabulous array of tropical fish.

Chetumal ★

The last, most important place on this road is Chetumal. Once a Mayan port for shipping cacao and gold, it now attracts plenty of Belizian tourists and some holiday-makers from Cancún. The highlight of the town is the **Museo de la Cultura Maya** and, if you have a car, there are plenty of Mayan ruins in the surrounding area.

Above: *The ruins at Tulum overlook the turquoise waters of the Caribbean from whence the conquistadors once arrived and changed the history of Mexico.*

CHOCOLATE MONEY

Such was the value the **Maya** placed on chocolate that **cocoa beans** were used as a form of **currency** during the Classical era (AD600–900). These valuable beans, fruit of a smallish tree, were culti-vated in parts of Quintana Roo, Chiapas and Guatemala. Today, chocolate plays an important role in Mexican cuisine in the form of *mole poblano*, the famous dish from Puebla, and also in hot chocolate drinks.

The Yucatán at a Glance

Nov to **Apr** is best. Rains fall in Apr–May and Sept–Jan. Tropical interior is always hot and fairly humid. Temperatures rarely below 27°C (81°F). Carnival (six weeks before Easter) is rather riotous on Cozumel. Christmas, Easter and US holidays see influxes of tourists. Divers find that the best season is Aug to Nov.

Cancún and Cozumel receive international **flights** from the USA and local flights from the capital and Mérida. Mérida, Campeche, Chetumal and Isla Mujeres have airports. **Buses** connect Mexico City with Cancún (22 hours), Mérida and Campeche (20 hours) and Chetumal (24 hours). Coastal buses go between Cancún and Tulum. **Ferries** make the 30-minute crossing some 14 times daily each way between Cozumel and Playa del Carmen.

Buses run between towns, taxis in main towns. Many towns are small enough to walk around. In the Yucatán, **rent a car** and drive yourself. You can do a one-way hire between Mérida and Cancún via Chichén Itzá.

There are hundreds of hotels in this area. Most are new and luxurious: budget ones are very hard to find. Expect to settle for rather expensive lodgings.

The sites of Tulum, Chichén Itzá and Uxmal all have lodges and hotels in the vicinity.

LUXURY

Ramada Hotel Campeche, Av Ruiz Cortines 51, Campeche, tel: (981) 62233, fax: 11618. Luxury overlooking the Gulf of Mexico.

Fiesta Americana Condesa, Paseo Kukulcán Km 16, Cancún, tel: (98) 85-1000, fax: 85-1800. Mexican luxury on the shoreline. Also two other Fiesta Americana hotels in Cancún.

Caesar Park Cancún Beach & Golf Resort, Paseo Kukulcán Km 17, Cancún, tel: (98) 81-8000, fax: 81-8080. Huge hotel combining large stretch of beach and 18-hole golf course.

Fiesta Americana Cozumel Reef, Km 7.5 south, Cozumel, tel: (987) 22622, fax: 22666. Beachside, just south of town. Particularly good for divers.

Presidente InterContinental, Km 6.5 south, Cozumel, tel: (987) 20322, fax: 21360. South of town, opposite small beach.

Fiesta Americana Mérida, Paseo de Montejo 451, Mérida, tel: (99) 42-1111. In keeping with colonial mansions in city.

La Posada del Capitán Lafitte, Km 62, Playa del Carmen, tel and fax: (987) 30212. Rustic luxury, just north of Playa on unspoiled beach.

El Faro, Calle 10 Norte, Playa del Carmen, tel: (987) 30970, fax: 30968. Delightfully private beachfront hotel.

Chichan Baal Kah, Av 18 Norte & Av Quinta, Playa del Carmen, tel and fax: (987) 31252. Very comfortable self-catering apartments.

MID-RANGE

Hotel Baluartes, Av Ruiz Cortines, Campeche, tel: (981) 66822, fax: 62410. An older, comfortable hotel, sea views.

María de Lourdes, Esq Orquidsas & Av Yaxchilán, Cancún Town, tel: (98) 84-4744, fax: 84-1242. Medium-sized family-run hotel.

Casablanca Playa, Calle 8 Norte, Playa del Carmen, tel: (987) 30057, fax: 30699. Airy clean rooms, central location.

Pelicano Inn, Calle 8 and beachfront, Playa del Carmen, tel: (987) 30997, fax: 30998. Beach hotel and restaurant.

Casa del Balam, Calle 60 no. 488, Mérida, tel: (99) 24-8844, fax: 24-5011. Old-world small hotel filled with antiques.

BUDGET

Hotel Colonial, Calle 14 no. 122, Campeche, tel: (981) 62222. A former mansion with simple rooms.

Hotel Dolores Alba, Calle 63 no. 464, Mérida, tel: (99) 21-3745. Excellent value with pool.

Posada d'Margo, Calle 10 Norte & 5a Av, Playa del Carmen, tel: (987) 30492. Simple, clean hotel, central.

Hotel Flamingo, Calle 6 Norte, San Miguel, Cozumel, tel and fax: (987) 21264. Good hotel, central location.

The Yucatán at a Glance

LUXURY
The Plantation House, Km 10.5, Kukulcán Blvd, Cancún, tel: (98) 83-1433. Lagoon-side, excellent Caribbean cuisine.
El Mexicano, by Plaza Caracol, Cancún, tel: (98) 83-2122. Mexican cuisine with Mariachi music and Ballet Folklórico.

MID-RANGE
Restaurant Marganzo, Campeche, facing Baluarte de la Soledad. Seafood cafés and restaurants abound in town.
Captain's Cove, Km 16, Kukulcán Blvd, Cancún, tel: (98) 85-0016. Seafoods and excellent buffet breakfasts.
Lorenzillo's, Km 10.5, Kukulcán Blvd, Cancún, tel: (98) 83-1254. Seafoods and fish.
Blue Parrot, 5a Av & 12 Norte, Playa del Carmen, tel: (987) 30083. Mexican cuisine.
Blue Lobster, 5a Av between 4 & 6 Norte, Playa del Carmen, tel: (987) 33360. Seafood, international and Mexican.
El Pirata, between 10th and 12th, on the beach, Playa del Carmen. Mexican, international.
El Capi Navegante, 312 Av 10 Sur, Cozumel, tel: (987) 21730. Delicious seafoods.
Ernesto's Fajitas Factory, 141 Rafael E. Melgar, Cozumel, tel: (987) 21575. Popular fajitas and other Mexican dishes.

BUDGET
Los Almendros, Calle 57 & 50, Mérida, tel: (99) 23-8135. Delicious Yucatecan cuisine.

In Campeche, **Casa de Arte-sanías** has a good selection of Yucatán handicrafts. The malls in the **Zona Hotelera** in Cancún are full of designer label clothing, jewellery and sports items. Select souvenirs from the Ki Huic market in Cancún Town, or in the Plaza Caracol. Try **Mercado Municipal** in Mérida for hammocks (also at **La Poblana**), embroidered blouses and hats, and the **Casa de Artesanías**, Calle 63, no. 503, tel: (99) 28-6676.

Nature lovers can take tours with **Ecoturismo Yucatán**, Mérida, tel: (99) 25-2187, a company that specializes in nature and archaeology. Visit Sian Ka'an on tours organized through **Amigos de Sian Ka'an**, Cancún, tel: (98) 84983. Trips to **Tulum**, **Chichén Itzá**, **Izamal** and other archaeological sites are easy to arrange. All the large hotels have tour desks which will fix up a tour.

US Consulates
Cancún: Plaza Caracol, 3rd Floor, Zona Hotelera, tel: (98) 83-0272.

Mérida: Paseo de Montejo 453, tel: (99) 25-5409.
British Consulates
Cancún: Royal Caribbean, Zona Hotelera, tel: (98) 85-1166 ext 462.
Mérida: Calle 53, no. 489, tel: (99) 28 2962.
Tourist Offices
Campeche: Calle 12, no. 153, tel: (981) 19255.
Mérida: Calle 59 n 54 (between 62 & 64), tel: (99) 28-6547.
Cancún: 26 Av Tulum, tel: (98) 84-6531.
Playa del Carmen: Av Juárez.
Cozumel: Plaza del Sol, 2nd Floor, tel: (987) 31001.
Dive Operators
AquaWorld, Km 15.2, Kukulcán Blvd, Cancún, tel: (98) 85-2288.
The Abyss Divers, Blue Parrot Inn, Playa del Carmen, Calle 12, tel: (987) 32164.
Dive Paradise, 601 Av Melgar, Cozumel, tel: (987) 21007.
Prodive, 198 Adolfo Rosado Salas Av 5, Cozumel, tel: (987) 24123.
Golf Courses
Pok-Ta-Pok Golf Course, tel: (98) 83-1277, fax: 83-3358.
Caesar Park Golf Course, tel: (98) 81-8000, fax:81-8080.

CANCÚN	J	F	M	A	M	J	J	A	S	O	N	D
AVERAGE TEMP. °F	74	75	78	79	83	84	84	84	83	81	78	80
AVERAGE TEMP. °C	23	24	25	26	28	29	29	29	28	27	25	26
RAINFALL in	0.8	1.3	1	1	2.5	3.5	2.5	2.8	4.5	7	7	1.3
RAINFALL mm	20	33	25	25	63	88	63	71	114	178	178	33

Travel Tips

Tourist Information

Mexico has a number of overseas tourist offices and ministries. **United Kingdom:** London, tel: (0171) 734-1058; **USA:** New York, tel: (212) 755-7261; Los Angeles, tel: (310) 203-8191; Washington, tel: (202) 728-1750; **Canada:** Toronto, tel: (416) 925-0704; Vancouver, tel: (604) 669-2485; **France:** Paris, tel: (01) 42 86 56 30; **Germany:** Frankfurt-am-Main, tel: (069) 25-2413; **Spain:** Madrid, tel: (91) 561-3520.

In Mexico City, SECTUR offers a 24-hour, 7-day a week number for advice or information, tel: (5) 250-0123. All major Mexican towns have tourist offices.

Entry Requirements

EU, **Australian**, **New Zealand**, **Norwegian**, **Swiss**, **Japanese** and **Argentinian** passport holders need a valid passport with over six months left before its expiry date. **US** and **Canadian** citizens need proof of citizenship with a photo attached. Citizens of most other countries, including South Africa and Eastern Europe, need visas from their local consulates or embassies. On arrival visitors need a **Tourist Card**. Forms available at airports or border crossings; these must be validated (valid for 90 days).

Customs

For importation of cars, *see* Getting There. Air travellers are given a customs declaration on arrival and the traveller then goes through one of the 'nothing to declare' or 'goods to declare' exits. Random searches are customary. Maximum customs allowance for adults includes 3 litres alcohol or wine, 400 cigarettes or 50 cigars, and 12 rolls of film. Personal effects, free of charge. Infringement of these regulations incur penalties.

Health Requirements

No vaccinations are required but various hazards exist. Sanitation practices are poor, generally, so various measures should be observed to reduce infection. Do *not* drink water from taps. Drink *only* sealed, bottled mineral water. Do *not* eat street food. Avoid ice in cool drinks. The most frequent complaint is '**Moctezuma's** revenge', or diarrhoea. Pharmacies sell plenty of remedies; take your own. If the problem persists in Mexico, consult a doctor. Mexico City is polluted. **Asthma** and respiratory sufferers should consult their doctor before arriving and bring all their medications. Toilets are not always well maintained except in smart hotels and restaurants. Those travelling to **tropical areas** where malaria is usually endemic should either bring a prophylactic or ensure they are covered with long sleeves and trousers every evening. Suitable clothing is considered just as effective as medication. Mexico City is at an altitude of 2240m (7350ft), Chihuahua, Zacatecas, Morelia, Guanajuato and Guadalajara are also towns at altitude. This can sometimes cause slight **altitude sickness** in the form of breathlessness or slight headache, until acclimatized. Relax on arrival and drink plenty of (nonalcoholic) beverages. An aspirin or paracetamol and a good night's sleep usually helps. Snorkellers and **scuba divers** are well advised to ensure their tetanus vaccinations are up to date. Coral cuts and scrapes are notoriously infectious. Selective driving of private cars is practiced on certain weekdays (not weekends) in Mexico City, to reduce **pollution emissions**. This does not affect visitors with their own cars.

Getting There

By Air: The national carrier, **Aeroméxico**, has direct fights to Mexico City from three cities in Europe and some 35 cities in North America. It also has direct flights from some American cities to Cancún, Guadalajara, Hermosillo, Mazatlán and Puerto Vallarta. Aeroméxico can also handle onward connections within the country to other cities. **Mexicana**, the predominantly domestic airline serves some destinations in the US. Many travellers, where direct connections are not possible or too expensive, fly via a US gateway (Los Angeles, Tucson, Houston or San Diego).

By Car: Travelling south by private vehicle, border crossings can be slow and complex. You can bring a car in from the US, but Mexican auto insurance and a Temporary Car Importation Permit both have to be obtained in advance. Offices of the American Automobile Association (AAA) can handle this, and so can Sanborn's Mexico Insurance Company toll-free in US (800) 222-0158. Cars rented from San Diego, with the express purpose of being used in Mexico, have completed these processes. For **car rental**, *see* Getting Around.

By Boat: It is possible to sail from Europe to Mexico on a passenger-carrying **cargo ship**. The crossing takes 2–3 weeks: it is an expensive but interesting option. The alternative is to visit Mexico on a **cruise ship**, of which there are dozens. Check with a travel agent.

What to Pack

Much of Mexico is at an altitude. Temperatures drop at night to as little as 12°C (54°F) in Mexico City, Guadalajara or Guanajuato even in June, July or August. In winter, **night temperatures** can hover around 6°C (43°F). Take a jacket for evenings and a woollen pullover. Shorts and skimpy clothing are for beach resorts only. Mexicans are very **traditional** in this respect and expect visitors to dress appropriately in all religious buildings. For business evenings, women should wear a dress, a man, jacket and tie. Hikers and **walkers** (even in archaeological areas) should always bring decent shoes or boots and socks to protect against insects and the occasional snake. Be aware of the dangers of **sun**. Sunshine at altitude, tropical beaches and desert areas are merciless on human skin. Hats, strong sun creams and long-sleeved shirts are recommended, especially for children.

Money Matters

The currency is the Peso, abbreviated to P. The currency is allowed to float by the government. Travellers will find that **US dollars cash** (particu-larly in smaller denominations) are the greatest standby whereas Pounds Sterling or Euros are not so easy to exchange. Banks (Banimex or Bancomer are the largest) and **casas de cambio** (exchange booths which often handle transactions faster than banks) will change **traveller's cheques**. Dollar cheques are advised. **ATMs** now abound in all cities making a quick and convenient way to access money. The most widely accepted **credit cards** are VISA and MasterCard. American Express is not that widely accepted. Do not carry more cash than you need at a time.

Accommodation

There are hotels for all budgets in Mexico. It is possible, still, to travel on US$25 a day but it is difficult. Cheap hostels, including **youth hostels** – under the management of Agencia Nacional de Juvenil, tel: (5) 5535-1605 – exist for

PUBLIC HOLIDAYS
1 January • New Year's Day
6 January • Epiphany
5 February • Constitution Day
21 March • Anniversary of Juárez' birthday
Easter Sunday
1 May • May Day
5 May • Fifth of May
16 September • Independence Day
12 October • Day of the Race
20 November • Anniversary of the Mexican Revolution
25 December • Christmas Day

GOOD READING

Greene, Graham (1969) *The Power and the Glory* (Penguin).
Lawrence, DH (1995) *The Plumed Serpent* (Wordsworth).
Lowry, Malcolm (1990) *Under the Volcano* (Picador).
Ortiz, Elizabeth Lambert (1992) *A Taste of Mexico* (Kyle Cathie).
Parkes, HB (1991) *History of Mexico* (Payot).
Riding, Alan (1985) *Distant Neighbors: a portrait of the Mexicans* (Knopf).

US$7 a bed, but you should generally allow a minimum of US$20 for budget accommodation, US$60 for moderate and US$110 and over for expensive. Mexico also has a super-expensive category. These are over US$270 per night (Los Cabos area, for instance). Apart from the international hotel chains (such as Meliá, Sheraton, Best Western, Westin, Hilton, Marriott, Holiday Inn/Crowne Plaza, Nikko) which are present in the capital as well as in other tourist destinations, the country has some excellent Mexican hotel chains which vary from moderate to ultraluxurious. Contact Fiesta Americana or Fiesta Real, Camino Real, Quinta Real, Calinda for information on their city and resort hotels. All are on the internet.

Eating Out

Mexicans eat their main meal in the middle of the day. In town, business is often conducted over long lunches. **Breakfasts** are between 08:00 and 11:00 (in larger city hotels they tend to be buffet-style), **lunch** from 14:00–16:00, and **dinner** starts at 21:00 (though many restaurants are open earlier) and can go on until 24:00 in the city. It is tempting to try Mexican street food. At best it can be delicious and healthy, but too often the results are disastrous. Choose a **taco stand** with care. If it is well-patronized with locals, then it is likely to be fine, taste and healthwise. *Comedores* are cheap eateries, often found around markets. Restaurants often offer a **comida corrida**, or daily menu: good value at US$5–12. Some chains (McDonalds, Kentucky Fried Chicken and Hard Rock Café) are found in the most touristy destinations. Mexican chains such as VIPS and Sanborn's also offer good food for reasonable prices. More upmarket places to eat include the Mexican chain restaurants Señor Frog and Carlos 'n' Charlie's.

Mexican food is usually spicy for European tastes although more spices and chillies are offered to beef it up further.

Vegetarians fare well in the large cities and tourist resorts but will have to supplement menus with market-bought food in the more rural areas. Lastly, delicious though it may be, fish and seafood can be a hazard if it is not superfresh.

Transport

Air: Aeropuerto International Benito Juárez is the main point of arrival and departure for international and domestic flights. It is only 5km (3 miles) east of downtown. Travelers with a minimum of luggage can use the Metro otherwise **prepaid official airport taxis** (yellow ones) from the airport are advised. Journey time to or from airport 20–45 minutes, depending on traffic.

There are over 50 domestic airports in the country. Aeroméxico, Mexicana, Aerolitoral and Aero California run domestic flights. Before leaving home, check what air passes exist for domestic flights. Bought before departing, these can offer considerable savings.

There is a departure tax (currently around US$18) from all airports for both domestic and international flights.

Road: Bringing in a vehicle is dealt with above. Driving in Mexico is on the right side of the road and road signs are international. There are now *autopista* toll roads in many parts of the country. A *cuota*, or toll, is payable. *Carreteras principales* are the main roads, *caminos* or *carreteras segundarias*, secondary roads and generally to be avoided. Mexico has a system of free breakdown assistance called **Angeles Verdes**, Green Angels. Besides checking for forest fires, road maintenance requirements and handing out traffic fines, they can fix broken down engines, give advice and medical assistance on over 60,000km (37,284 miles) of roads daily. Their Mexico City number is (5) 250-8221.

Various **hazards** exist which should be noted:

• It is inadvisable to drive **after dark**.

• **Roadworks** are sometimes signalled only by a scattering of stones around working area.

• **Animals** (and rural humans) wander idly across roads.

• **Speed bumps** exist in towns to slow vehicles down.

• Use of **flashing indicator lights** outside major towns is not always the same as back home. If you need to turn and cross traffic, it is advisable to pull off the road on the right, then cross when all is clear.

• **Lock all doors** in town traffic and when leaving your car. **Car rental** is possible in many cities including Cancún, Playa del Carmen, Mérida, Acapulco, Ixtapa, Puerto Vallarta, La Paz, Mazatlán, Tijuana and Los Cabos. Hertz, Avis, Thrifty and Budget are big in the country but other small, less expensive companies exist in each town. **Buses:** Mexico has a great network of intercity buses. There are three categories: deluxe, first- and second-class. **Deluxe** and **first-class** take roughly the same time for journeys but differ in price and comfort; **second-class** takes longer and

costs less. In large cities buses depart from different bus **terminals**, depending on the direction of journey and the terminals are usually out of the centre of town. For longer journeys and deluxe buses, **reserve** seats and pay in advance. If you are city-hopping by bus, buy the **onward ticket** on arrival to save time. **Trains:** The *Ferrocariles Nacionales de México* (FNM) serve some of the larger cities in the country but are slow. There is ***primera preferente***, first class, and ***segunda***, second class. On some routes (Ciudad Juárez, Guadalajara, Veracruz or Monterrey) a ***coche dormitorio***, or sleeping car, is available at a supplement. A restaurant car is also available. The **Chihuahua al Pacífico** train that passes through the Barranca del Cobre is a popular train for tourists and the most spectacular ride in the country.

Business Hours

Standard hours are 09:00–18:30, with a 1–2 hour lunch break. Government offices are open 08:30–15:00 and

often 18:00–21:00; banks 09:00–14:30, some also 16:00–18:00. Casas de Cambio are open longer hours. Shops open around 10:00 and close between 19:00 and 21:00.

Time Difference

Mexico has three time zones. Mexico City and most of central Mexico is on **Hora del Centro**. This is GMT minus 6 hours in winter, and GMT minus 5 in summer (first Sunday in April to last Sunday in October). Baja California Sur, Sinaloa, Sonora and Nayarit are on **Horas de las Montañas** (GMT minus 7 hours in winter, minus 6 in summer). Baja California Norte is on **Hora del Pacífico**. This is GMT minus 8 hours in winter, and minus 7 in summer.

Communications

The international **telephone** dialling code for Mexico is 52. Each town has a prefix or area code. For example Mexico City is (5), Los Cabos (114) and Cancún (98). To call within a

CONVERSION CHART		
FROM	TO	MULTIPLY BY
Millimetres	Inches	0.0394
Metres	Yards	1.0936
Metres	Feet	3.281
Kilometres	Miles	0.6214
Square kilometres	Square miles	0.386
Hectares	Acres	2.471
Litres	Pints	1.760
Kilograms	Pounds	2.205
Tonnes	Tons	0.984
To convert Celsius to Fahrenheit: x 9 ÷ 5 + 32		

city, dial the number only without area code. To call from one city to another, add (01) before the area code. To make overseas calls, dial 00 + country code + area code + number. *Caseta de teléfono*, or public phones, usually use *tarjeta telefónicas* (phone cards), on sale in many shops or kiosks.
Home Country Direct (*País Directo*) is worthwhile using if you need to call home. AT&T, MCI, Sprint and British Telecom have their own access numbers. Check these before leaving.
Post Offices are open 08:30–14:30. Air mail can take a long time, so urgent packages should be sent by **courier**. Services by DHL, UPS and Federal Express are all available.

Electricity
Mexico's voltage is 125 volts at 60 hertz. If your electrical equipment is 220v you will need an adapter.

Weights and Measures
Mexico uses the metric system.

Health Services
Major medical problems, or accidents, can be treated at **ABC Hospital**, tel: (5) 230-8000, or 230-8161 for emergencies. Medical costs are generally low in Mexico. Emergency pharmacies such as **Sanborn's**, Paseo de la Reforma 333, tel: (5) 525-7545, are open 18 hours a day.

Personal Safety
Much has been written about the rising crime in Mexico, particularly in the capital. It exists but it doesn't have to ruin a

holiday. Petty crime on public transport is rife. Take precautions generally and especially in Mexico City where we advise:
• Do not walk alone at night.
• Never hail a taxi on the street. Take one from a *sitio* (taxi rank) or call a reputable radio taxi.
• Do not carry a bag or rucksack that could be snatched.
• Do not show cash in public places and take good care of fancy cameras.
• Leave the best jewellery at home. Mexico has plenty of pretty inexpensive items.
• Beware of guides who approach you.
• If renting a car, do not drive at night. Roads are lethal and the driving, often without headlights, erratic.

Emergencies
Call **08** or emergency English-speaking tourist service at tel: (5) 250-0123. For **medical** emergencies, call ABC Hospital, tel: (5) 230-8161. Embassies: USA, tel: (5) 211-0042; Australian, tel: (5) 531-5225; British, tel: (5) 207-2089; Canadian, tel: (5) 724-7900.

Etiquette
Mexicans are very traditional and expect decent dress and manners. Hand shaking is important. A *buenos días* (good morning), *hastaluego* (goodbye) and *gracias* (thank you) are always appreciated when appropriate. Nude and topless sunbathing are against the law.

Tipping
Tipping is part of life in Mexico and encourages decent service. Waiters should

be tipped 10 per cent. Hotel porters should receive approx. US$1 per person. Tipping a taxi is not customary but if his service was exceptional, a small tip would be kind.

Language
The official language in Mexico is Spanish. English is widely spoken in the resorts and in Mexico City.

USEFUL PHRASES

Good day • *Buenos días*
Good afternoon •
Buenas tardes
Good evening •
Buenas noches
Excuse me (passing someone)
• *Con Permiso*
Excuse me (sorry) •
Discúlpame
With great pleasure •
Con mucho gusto
Many thanks • *Muchas Gracias*
You're welcome • *De nada*
Do you speak English? •
¿Habla usted inglés?
Okay • *Vale* (pronounced like 'ballet')
Hello • *¡Hola!*
How much is ... ? •
¿Cuánto cuesta ... ?
It is rather expensive •
Es muy caro
What is your best price? •
¿Cual es su último precio?
What time does it leave/arrive in ...? • *¿A que hora sale/llega a ... ?*
Fill up the tank, please •
Llénelo, por favor
Menu, please • *La carta, por favor*
Purified water without ice, please • *Agua purificada, sin hielo, por favor*

INDEX